Couples Therapy Workbook

Move From Struggle to Connection – Improve Communication, Trust, and Intimacy in Your Relationship

Chloe Slater

Table of Contents

Introduction

Being in love can be one of the best things in the world. Opening your heart and life to another person takes a lot of vulnerability and courage. But, as Christopher McCandless said, "Happiness is only real when shared." This was one of the last things that the intrepid young traveler realized after rejecting society and living alone in the wilderness, before also dying alone. I often think of this quote and my initial trepidations when it came to love. As someone who was once very closed off from the idea of sharing my life with someone else, particularly with entrusting them with a large portion of my heart, and giving them access to my time and feelings, I too have grown to realize that the great highs (and the lows) of life are better when shared with someone you care about, who provides you with the same reassurance and stable love.

Although family and friends can provide an incredibly supportive network, romantic love is different. Finding the right person to love is also incredibly difficult. You would think it is easier in today's world, where you can browse nearby singles at the click of a button, give someone's selfie a double tap, and bravely attend a speed-dating night. However, finding reliable and trusted partners is still a struggle (probably enough for a whole new book).

Early Relationship Stages

If you have found a partner and a loved one, are confident in your future together, and enjoy spending time together, it can sometimes feel like the end of the road. You have secured the bag. You have deleted the dating apps. You have hard-launched them on social media. But, as I too learned, this is not the case. Maintaining relationships and navigating life together, particularly as you grow and learn as a couple, is in itself a challenging and complex process that often requires far more thought and attention than we might initially realize.

I once boasted about the ease of my relationships. "No, we are just a couple who do not argue," I would respond with pity to my friends lamenting their relationship struggles. It was like we were made for each other. Soulmates, even. But, as our relationship grew and changed, the rose-tinted glasses faded away, and we both began to notice the shortcomings in the other and exhibit our flaws; things got a lot tougher. We began to argue, and having never argued before, we had no idea how to sort it out. I became increasingly anxious. If we were arguing, maybe we were not meant to be. The relationships we see in media, movies, and books, are often picture-perfect. Surely disagreements and being unable to see eye-to-eye meant my partner was not right for me.

When Things Start to Go Wrong

However, change and conflict are both natural parts of a growing relationship. Things often start blissfully. It is easy to bring your best self to your first date (and the first 6 months thereafter) and skim over the fact that you drink too much. Or that you are a very messy person. Or that you are desperately anxious. Or perhaps something deeply traumatic happened to you as a child, and you are still in therapy every week. However, as relationships grow and evolve, these elements tend to come out into play.

I once thought that conflict meant the doom of a relationship but have come to understand that this is not the case. Resolving arguments is a skill that takes practice. I have even regularly heard about the end of my friends' relationships who were in the same boat and never argued with their partners. In never arguing, they never learned how to resolve conflict, and thus when suddenly faced with a disagreement, had no idea how to navigate it or move forwards.

Communication

The same applies to communication. It is a skill that improves with practice. While you might talk regularly with your partner, how much are you saying? How much are they hearing? Talking is different from effectively communicating your ideas, thoughts, and feelings, and while it comes naturally to some, it takes a little practice for others. Regarded as the cornerstone for many relationships, communication was also one of the biggest 'make-or-break-it' of my own. A lot of our initial conflict stemmed from our inability to open up and listen to one another. There was a lot of cutting in, telling each other we were too sensitive, or being unable to see where the other person was coming from. However, with time, my partner and I have both worked on these skills and now move through communication and conflict with an ease that many of the couples I know personally struggle with.

As someone with an anxious attachment style, it has taken me years (and a great deal of research) to get to the place where I am now in my relationship and build a more secure attachment style. That still does not mean that it is the end of the road for me. I continue to nurture and put effort into my relationship every day, as does my partner, and we work together to learn more about each other and how we can best navigate life, sharing our happiness.

What You Will Get

As my journey took a great deal of ups and downs, and learning how to overcome these challenges, I hope that I will be able to impart this knowledge to you, so that you might be able to navigate these challenges better yourself. Relationships are a blessing and can bring so much joy and fulfillment to our lives, but can also involve a great deal of stress, worry, and pain. All forms of events and experiences that life throws our way can impact our relationships with our partners. Big life changes, the relationships around us, work and money, past trauma, and even infidelity. All of these issues can surface and be difficult to take on as a couple. But, the key to doing so is to approach it together, as a team.

In this book, I will be covering relationship issues. Not only will I be addressing the more challenging elements that you might be facing, or will face in the future, but I will also provide you with ways you can better connect with your partner and learn how you can both give and receive the love you both desire. By the end of the book, my goal is to provide you with a host of skills in dealing with relationship issues and get you and your partner on the same page, so that you can face every life issue head-on and enjoy your shared happiness.

Reading is not for everyone, so I have compiled my knowledge and research into shortcuts for learning many of the pathways I have covered myself. Learning with your partner is often best approached interactively, so I have incorporated multiple activities in each chapter for you to try. Whether you are reading this yourself, or as a couple, you will hopefully enjoy contemplating your answers to the questions provided, to help you reflect on your current relationship, your struggles, and how you can best resolve them.

Whether you are working through healing from a life-changing experience you experienced on your own or something your partner was involved with like cheating, whether you are just arguing about who has to walk the dog or wash the dishes, whether you feel like your partner is not managing to support you or is not making you feel appreciated daily, I have got the answers covered. By the end of this workbook, I hope to take you to a place where you have the skills needed to incorporate into your relationship and have the confidence that no matter the issue, you will be able to face it together and continue building a healthy and happy life.

Chapter 1:

What Is Love?

"Falling in love is more than infatuation. It is the need to feel whole, to feel safe, to be healed, to join together with someone, heart, and soul."

— Michael R. French

Maintaining Healthy Relationships

F alling in love is easy (or so the romcoms would have us believe). Even that is quite difficult nowadays, between hookup culture and app-dating and ghosting, breadcrumbing, texting games, and so on. Once you have bagged a partner, you might think the job is done, and you can rest now. However, keeping a relationship alive, keeping your love aflame, and continuing to work successfully together can often feel more difficult than having ignited the spark in the first place.

Healthy and long-lasting relationships take a lot of consistent work and nurturing in all the following categories:

Communication: Communication is often the lifeline and the heart of a successful and healthy relationship. It also goes beyond talking to one another, but rather actively listening to what the other person is saying, trying to understand their point of view, and taking it on board. Healthy communication involves a large degree of openness, being able to speak candidly about what you are feeling, and not being afraid of your partner acting in a hostile manner in response or judging you. It also involves cohesion in being able to speak and plan things so you are both on the same page.

Trust: Another incredibly important aspect of healthy relationships is trusting your partner. Trusting their faithfulness, trusting their actions, trusting they mean what they say. It is difficult to continue loving and growing with someone whom you do not trust.

Honesty: Hand in hand with trust comes honesty, which often leads to greater trust between people. Being honest about your feelings and your actions creates a space in which both people feel comfortable sharing their mindsets and trust that their partner will respect them.

Independence: Even when head over heels for your partner, feeling like you want to spend every second glued to their ribs is not a healthy approach. Continuing to grow your interests and enjoy hobbies and other aspects of life on your own allows two people to come together, rather than rely so strongly on one another that issues begin to arise out of co-dependency.

Support: Your partner should be your biggest cheerleader, and you should be theirs. When it comes to career, life goals, and daily struggles, being able to confide and share these with your partner is incredibly important. This might mean praise and congratulating or providing a shoulder you can lean on when times are tough and an ear that will commiserate with your struggles and support you through them.

Healthy Boundaries: Respecting one another's boundaries is also a large factor in successful and healthy relationships. This involves asking for your partner's consent and respecting their wishes, knowing their limits, and respecting these boundaries.

Feeling Safe: Feeling safe with your partner is a vital element to being able to share your feelings openly and being able to trust that they have your best interests at heart.

Enjoyment: Even after years in a relationship, where you are both settled into a routine, you should still enjoy the time spent together and have fun in your interactions.

Building a healthy relationship that incorporates all of the above is often not easy. It also seems arduous after a peaceful and easy honeymoon period. Everything was rose-tinted and blissful after you first met, and then you are suddenly arguing over who has to unload the dishwasher. Long-lasting and successful relationships take time. Going through ups and downs with your partner is not uncommon, but a willingness to grow and learn, and to adapt and accommodate your partner is important. The key is after all in the word; partners, meaning that you have to work and grow together to find fulfilling and long-lasting happiness.

The key to tackling these goals together and remaining on the same page in your relationship is openness and willingness to learn. Conflict is bound to happen. Avoiding all arguments is often less productive than being able to bring up and discuss issues as they arise, as avoiding conflict can lead to deep-seated resentment. Maybe you are upset that your partner spends a lot of the weekends golfing when you are left home with all the housework, but you do not want to bring it up because you love them and you do not want to seem needy. But your frustration grows as the chores mount up, and you end up exploding at them for leaving a pair of socks in the kitchen. Approaching conflict calmly and securely and having the confidence to engage in respectful disagreement also teaches you how both you and your partner deal with conflict, and successful ways to mediate and resolve.

Keeping the Spark Alive

Falling in love is easy, staying in love, is not quite such a smooth ride. It is easy to let your romantic feelings for one another take a back seat when life gets in the way. Work, children, and other commitments compete for your attention, and you drift away from spending time together on an emotional level – only coming together when issues arise. However, keeping your 'spark' alive is key to the longevity of your relationship, and requires frequent attention to avoid running into bigger issues down the line.

To Do so, Spend Quality Time Together: Setting aside time away from distractions, putting your phone down and your work aside, and giving your partner your full attention will help to nurture your feelings for one another. This is often a step beyond watching television together or running to the grocery store. Engage in regular date nights when possible, and partake in hobbies or interests you both share. Try new things to bring something exciting and interesting to your life which you can discuss later, and work on building new positive memories together throughout your relationship.

Remember to Also Work on Your Communication: Your partner is not a mind reader. Do not be afraid of telling them how you feel, what you need, and how they could better support you. Practice active listening when they speak to you, always showing openness through body language and keeping any rash judgment to yourself. A relationship functions best when both parties can listen and share and then work through potential solutions together. If one person feels criticized or judged, they may refrain from sharing in the future, which can cause resentment and anger to grow.

Additionally, Keep Your Love Life Alive: Physical intimacy does not just have to mean sex, but be mindful that this can be forced onto the back burner of priorities in busy shared lives, so set time aside to keep your physical connection. Additionally, work on showing your affection through other physical gestures. Hand-holding, hugging, and kissing all work to solidify and reassure your partner of your affection.

Remember to Work Together, Not Apart: Relationships are rarely split 50/50. You might find yourself putting in more effort while your partner is preoccupied or vice versa. Be mindful of the other priorities you both have in life and allow flexibility to ensure that you both can focus on what is important as well as your love for one another. Relationships are not a case of winning either. When conflict arises, avoid approaching it with the mindset of having to win an argument and take down your partner. Conflict, while inevitable, needs to be approached with a mindset of working together to solve problems, so you can both function in the smoothest way possible. Avoid attacking your partner's weak spots in the heat of the moment as hurtful things cannot be taken back, and instead learn to manage your stress and emotions to avoid letting them spill out into your love life.

Foster Your Interests While Being in a Relationship: Continuing to work on your interests, developing your hobbies, and otherwise spending time apart will mean you feel at ease with yourself and can bring self-confidence and self-love to your relationship with your partner. While you might enjoy one another's company, not everything should be done together.

Finally, Relationships Come With a Lot of Ups and Downs: You might find that the downs last longer the longer you are together. You might also reflect on how idyllic the first year of your relationship was and wonder where it all went wrong. However, accept that all relationships go through highs and lows. Outside factors like work stress, grief, health issues, or plenty of others can affect your interactions with your partner. Avoid running for the hills as soon as it gets a little tough. Life is hard, as are relationships. Feeling like you have to work a little harder for some time is natural, and part of the grift of successful long-term relationships. Not everything will be happy and easy and carefree, but knowing how to communicate and support your partner when times are tough will ensure that you get through these tough times together.

Is My Relationship Healthy?

It is worth checking in on your relationship every so often to assess whether you and your partner are both satisfied and if you are both meeting the following needs for each other. These questions also apply in reverse; how might your partner respond to them considering how you treat them, and is there anything you could do differently to improve your relationship?

Do you feel like your partner listens to you?

_____

_____

_____

Do you feel comfortable sharing things that your partner has said or done that might have upset you?

_____

_____

_____

Do you enjoy spending time together?

_____

_____

Does your partner support your accomplishments?

_____

_____

Does your partner make an effort with your friends and family?

_____

_____

_____

Does your partner respect and allow for your opinion if it differs from theirs?

_____

_____

_____

Does your partner encourage you to spend time with friends and family, and to pursue your interests?

_____

_____

_____

Healthy relationships come with many benefits. Having an encouraging and supportive partner can improve your self-worth and confidence, can provide you with a safe space and help you to feel less lonely, and can encourage you to try new things, both with your partner and alone, to allow you to grow individually and as a couple.

How Can I Communicate Effectively With My Partner?

Communication is a skill. It comes naturally to some, for others, it takes work and practice. Communication also enables you to share openly with your partner and allows them to share with you. This fosters an environment of trust and can mean that any issues are raised and dealt with quickly. Consider the following when communicating with your partner to encourage hearing and understanding each other better:

- Give your partner your full attention, put your phone away, and paraphrase or ask questions to show that you are listening.
- Be mindful of your body language. Use eye contact and open body language to encourage them to share.
- Avoid trying to mind read or expecting your partner to do so. Explain how you feel and the reasons behind your feelings.
- Be honest and avoid lying or skirting around issues.
- Do not interrupt them when they are talking.
- Be respectful when listening to your partner's point of view, even if you do not agree.
- Avoid being overly defensive or retaliating if you feel hurt.

How Can I Improve My Relationship?

Maintaining healthy relationships means less stress and more ability to focus on other issues. It also provides you with a more positive mood and outlook on life, improves your general well-being, and generally includes factoring the following into your life:

Prioritize Your Relationship: Avoid letting your relationship slip out of your priorities, even if life is busy. Set time aside to spend quality time with one another, by putting away distractions and going on date nights.

Find Shared Interests: Finding new hobbies that you both enjoy can provide opportunities for bonding, and can give you a shared interest to look forward to.

Communicate: If something is upsetting you, tell your partner why. Avoid engaging in silent treatment or acting in a passive-aggressive manner when upset instead of explaining why you are feeling this way and trying to work through the issue.

Say Sorry When You Are in the Wrong: If you hurt your partner by saying something or doing something to upset them, own up when you are in the wrong. A heartfelt apology can go a long way and will prevent resentment from building up.

Compromise: As two individuals, you will be bound to disagree over certain things. Be willing to accommodate your partner's needs and be flexible in finding a middle ground to sort out disagreements, and expect the same flexibility in return.

Show Your Affection: Remind your partner regularly of your love and show them your affection. Love languages vary, but try to gauge how your partner best receives your affection – whether hugs and kisses, small gifts, or acts of service like bringing them a coffee (this will be explored in Chapter 3).

Work on Yourself: Avoid letting your stress filter out into your relationship. Avoid also putting your partner above everything else in your life and losing sight of yourself. Develop and nurture your interests and relationships outside of your partner to continue to be able to grow as an individual.

The Importance of Setting Boundaries

By 'boundaries' you probably think of a fence or a wall, or something that prevents you from going from one area to another. However, boundaries are often not something negative, but rather what you put in place as means of self-control to protect yourself and show what your limits are.

Healthy Boundaries:

- Encourage independence.
- Set expectations.
- Ensure you are physically and emotionally safe.
- Provide yourself with self-respect and confidence.
- Distinguish your own needs from those around you.

Unhealthy boundaries tend to vary between boundaries that are too rigid, or boundaries that are too weak. They can lead to numerous issues in relationships, such as poor self-esteem if a friend or partner repeatedly makes you feel uncomfortable or taken advantage of. Equally, pushing someone else's boundaries can damage a relationship as you both lose respect for one another and cause resentment to flourish.

Defining your boundaries is sometimes difficult, and varies immensely from person to person. What one person deems acceptable might be too much or not enough for another. For example, you might be so desperate to find and keep someone's affection that you lose all self-control and let them walk all over you by pushing your boundaries and making you feel uncomfortable. Equally, you might be so careful of your heart and emotions and so protective of yourself that you build boundaries so tightly around yourself and do not let anyone in out of fear of hurting you. Finding a middle ground of what your boundaries are is difficult, but also key to maintaining successful relationships.

Types of Boundaries

Personal boundaries vary in form but tend to be grouped within the following categories:

Physical Boundaries: Physical boundaries ensure you feel safe and that your personal space is protected. This can extend to your living space and privacy.

- I prefer handshakes over hugs.
- I do not want people going through my wardrobe.
- I do not want people to smoke in my house.

Emotional Boundaries: Setting emotional boundaries ensures that others respect your thoughts and feelings on certain subjects and encourage emotional safety and security. In setting emotional boundaries, you also take responsibility for your own emotions and separate your feelings from theirs.

- I do not want to discuss this subject.
- I do not want to be criticized for something that is beyond my control.
- I will not be spoken to in that way.

Sexual Boundaries: These set what you feel comfortable with what kind of intimacy you consent to, how often, and with whom.

- Saying no when you do not like something.
- Asking for consent.

Financial/Material Boundaries: Financial boundaries set what you are comfortable spending and what your limits are, and also help you set how others should treat your possessions.

- I am trying to save so I do not want to spend all my money on a holiday.
- I do not feel comfortable with you using my car.

Time Boundaries: These protect how you spend your time and help you avoid feeling overworked or taken advantage of.

- I cannot text you during the day when I am at work as I am busy.
- I need to be home in bed before 11 pm as I have work tomorrow.

Boundaries are also not set in stone and can shift, change, and adapt in relationships as people grow and their expectations change. If you do feel like something you consider a boundary is changing, be sure to voice this to your partner and explain the reasonings so that they do not unknowingly push you beyond what you are comfortable with.

How to Set and Maintain Healthy Boundaries

Ideally, you know what you are comfortable with, you set this early on, and your partner respects your boundaries. However, sometimes it takes time to realize what you are comfortable with and what your limits are. Consider the following when establishing your boundaries and defining how you will maintain them:

Consider What You Want in Your Relationship: Consider your core values and beliefs, what you admire in others, and what you need to feel comfortable.

Do you value your independence?

_____

_____

_____

How do you like to spend your time?

_____

_____

_____

What traits do you enjoy in other people?

_____

_____

_____

Consider How You Feel Around That Person: When setting certain boundaries with one individual, consider how they make you feel and if you then need to adapt certain boundaries in response to their behavior. Perhaps they made a joke you were uncomfortable with or pressured you to do something you did not like. Reflecting on these will help you set boundaries with that person to ensure you both feel comfortable moving forwards.

Communicate Your Needs: Avoid setting hard boundaries in your head but not communicating them to your partner, as they will likely be unaware if they do push this boundary. Use 'I' statements when conveying these to show that you are taking accountability for your emotions and explain your thought processes, for example, "I feel like you are disrespecting my time when you arrive late. Could you try and be more on time or at least text me to tell me you are running late,", instead of "You are always late and it is rude. You need to get your life together."

Enforce Your Boundaries: Even if you set and communicate your boundaries effectively, there will be occasions when these boundaries are disrespected, both intentionally and unintentionally. If this happens, remain calm and avoid reacting with heightened emotions. Calmly restate your boundaries in case the other person is not aware. Additionally, have consequences for crossing a boundary. It is important that you do follow through with the consequences if you do state them, and they are not just empty threats. For example, telling someone that you will end your relationship if they continue lying and then failing to do so will only demean your self-worth and cause you both to lose respect for one another.

Respecting Someone Else's Boundaries

Just as you have boundaries, your partner will too. It is important you respect these and act accordingly if you do cross them. You might personally be upset and feel ashamed if your partner tells you that you have disrespected them in some way, and feel the desire to defend yourself or tell them that they are overreacting. However, everyone is entitled to their own emotions and feels things differently, and your partner voicing a boundary is simply them telling you how to love them and ensure that they feel safe and protected.

If this does happen, listen attentively to what your partner is saying and what their boundary is. Accept that that person knows themselves best, and avoid assuming what their needs are for them. Apologize, when necessary, own up to your mistake, and reassure them that it will not happen in the future.

Friendship in Relationships

Ideally, your partner should also be your best friend. This means having a relationship outside of romance and sexual attraction, where you have unwavering support for one another, can laugh at each other's jokes, and enjoy spending time together. A healthy friendship is key to a long-lasting relationship and can be built through many of the same ways previously mentioned that seek to support relationships.

Spend Quality Time Together: Find shared interests and new interests, and dedicate regular time together away from distractions to nurture this bond.

Support One Another: Celebrate each other's wins and be the shoulder for your partner to lean on in their struggles.

Be Vulnerable: Open up, share your emotions and concerns, and work together to get through these feelings.

Recognize Your Differences and Enjoy Them: Maybe your partner sees differently on certain key topics. Rather than smiting them down, enjoy debating and seeing the world from someone else's perspective.

Voice Your Affection: Tell your partner what you like about them and affirm the qualities that you appreciate.

Fight Fair: Learning how to bring up disagreements and resolve conflict fairly is key to maintaining a healthy relationship.

Be Gentle: Empathize with your partner's issues and nurture one another through good and bad times.

Be Willing to Learn: Keeping an open mind and being ready to grow and change with a person will help you both evolve together.

Trust in Relationships

Trusting your partner, that they have your best interests at heart, that they are being honest, and that you can depend on them, is also a key part of having a long and fulfilling relationship. Trust is very difficult to rebuild once broken, as we will explore later in the book. However, the key pillars for building trust with your partner are as follows:

Honesty: Lying or being dishonest can ruin trust very quickly. Instead, being open with your feelings demonstrates that you value your partner and trust them and that they can depend on what you say.

Vulnerability: Opening up can be scary, but letting your guard down and showing your feelings will demonstrate mutual trust.

Communication: Being comfortable in telling your partner how you feel will put an end to doubt and overthinking, and encourage you both to be open and honest with your feelings.

Empathy: Showing you care about your partner's struggles will encourage them to confide and open up to you, showing that they can rely on you, even for issues that do not concern you directly.

Apologizing: When necessary, taking ownership of your mistakes and being able to apologize demonstrates to your partner that you can admit your wrongdoing and make amends for it.

Common Pitfalls in Relationships and How to Avoid Them

It is easy to make mistakes, and less easy to repair them. Nonetheless, be aware of some of the following areas in which you could damage your relationship, as being conscious of these will enable you to avoid slipping up and hurting yourself or your partner. If this does happen, do not be too hard on yourself or your partner, but be ready to apologize and rebuild any broken trust.

Taking Your Partner for Granted: Particularly in long-term relationships, it is easy to take your partner for granted and stop putting so much time and energy into keeping your relationship alive. However, if you do find yourself taking them for granted, consider what life might be like without them. If you do find yourself taking them for granted, consider what you can do to revive your affection and show how much you appreciate them.

Criticizing Your Partner to Your Friends and Loved Ones: It might be tempting to text a friend or parent about how irritating your partner is. However, this builds up resentment amongst your loved ones and will often not help sort out the issue. Bring up issues with your partner directly and work together to sort these out rather than only venting to outside individuals.

Not Taking Your Partner Seriously: Failing to prioritize your partner in your life and accommodate them and their feelings will leave them feeling disregarded and pushed aside.

Trying to Control Your Partner: It is okay to set boundaries, but trying to overly control your partner, telling them what they can and cannot do, and monitoring their every step will restrict them and leave them feeling stifled.

Avoiding All Confrontation: People rarely enjoy fighting, so it might be tempting to avoid bringing up issues and sweep them under the rug. However, this leads to resentment building up which can then boil over and cause huge arguments. Equally, bringing up issues and resolving them develops your conflict resolution skills together, which means you will be more capable of sorting out issues in the long run.

Expecting Your Partner to Be Perfect: Everyone makes mistakes. Failing to give your partner leniency when they do mess up and setting unrealistically high expectations is setting them up to fail.

Trying to Change Your Partner: You can set expectations and boundaries and bring up areas where your partner falls short, but everyone is unique. We are often drawn to people with different traits from us and might find over time that we want to make the person more like us. However, try and remember what drew you to this person in the first place, and accept that you have your differences.

Keeping Secrets: You do not have to share every minute detail of your life, but avoid keeping major life secrets or being dishonest with your partner as this will ruin your trust when it does eventually surface.

Becoming Too Co-Dependent: As two individuals, you should also lead independent lives. Becoming too dependent on one another causes issues as you rely too much on one another. Instead, seek to develop your hobbies and interests and come together as two halves of a whole.

Activities for Building a Healthy Relationship

Consider trying out one or more of the following to work on connecting with your partner and nurturing your emotional connection:

Outdoor Activities: Going hiking, for a road trip, camping, or whatever is to your fancy gets you out of the house to enjoy an activity beyond your normal routine with your partner.

Experience Something New Together: Even if you have been together for a while, participating in something new and exciting like an escape room or a skydive can give you both the thrill of adrenaline and something to get excited over.

Complete a Project Together: This can be as simple as cooking a new meal together that you have not tried to make before, taking up a gardening project, or setting a fitness goal like a regular run or marathon.

Share Books, Music, and Movies: You can watch, read, or listen to them together, or send your partner recommendations so that you can discuss them at a later point.

Create an Appreciation List: If there are lots of things you love about your partner, let them know. Write these down and share them with your partner to show how much you appreciate them and demonstrate your thoughtfulness.

Activities for Setting Boundaries

Sit down with your partner and pose the following questions. A deep dive can be at times awkward, but opening up and exploring one another's boundaries is often conducive to helping you both understand one another better.

What do you consider healthy boundaries in a relationship?

_____

_____

_____

_____

What are your values and beliefs, and do your boundaries reflect these values?

_____

_____

_____

_____

Who or what in your life has shaped your boundaries?

_____

_____

_____

_____

Boundary Setting Examples:

Setting and enforcing boundaries can be difficult, particularly for anxious or insecure individuals. Below are some examples of how to react and respond in a calm yet confident manner in situations where you might feel your boundaries are being pushed.

Example 1: Your partner enjoys staying up at night and wants you to watch the rest of a movie, but you are concerned about being overtired for work tomorrow.

Response: "I would love to finish it, but I do not want to be tired tomorrow so I am going to go to bed. I am happy to watch the rest tomorrow though."

Example 2: Your partner keeps teasing you about your fitness level, and it is making you self-conscious.

Response: "I have noticed that you have been making a few comments about my health and fitness. I appreciate that you are looking out for me and doing it in my best interest but could we avoid that topic as it is beginning to make me feel self-conscious."

Example 3: You have been trying hard to save to put a deposit on a house, but your partner loves expensive dinners and nights out. How do you bring up your financial concerns?

Response: I have enjoyed the dates we have been on recently and love spending time with you, but maybe we could work on our cooking skills at home? I think that would be a great way to save some money and build on our cooking skills since I am trying to save money.

Try it Yourself in the Questions Below:

Your partner calls and texts you while you are busy at work during the day. You appreciate their attention but need to enforce the fact that you do not need constant communication while at work, nor have time for it. How do you respond?

_____

_____

_____

_____

Your partner wants to get a pet ... NOW!!! You feel like it is an inappropriate point in your lives to get something that requires so much responsibility. How might you approach this conversation?

_____

_____

_____

_____

_____

You are on holiday with your partner and their family and friends. While enjoying your time, you do feel the need to recharge your social battery. How might you communicate your need for some respected time alone?

_____

_____

_____

_____

_____

Activities for Building Trust

Consider trying out one of the following activities with your partner to work on your trust skills together:

Make a Vision Board: Planning for the future can be a fun shared activity, and give you something to look forward to and to work for.

You will need:

- Old magazines
- Glue
- Scissors
- Cardboard
- Pens and decorations

Choose a theme. Examples might be your future home, life in 10 years, or the future of the human race. Have fun decorating the board and keep it somewhere in your home to reflect on your shared vision.

Cuddle: Hugging and cuddling encourage your body to release oxytocin, sometimes known as the love hormone. Set time aside without distractions in a quiet place and spend 10 – 20 minutes enjoying one another's company, snuggling, and touching in a non-erotic way.

Do a Trust Fall: Either with your eyes closed or a blindfold on, stand behind your partner and get them to cross their arms. Get them to slowly (and gently) fall backward into your arms, catching them before they hit the ground. Swap roles and demonstrate to one another that you will always be there to catch your partner.

Eye Gaze: Sit opposite your partner on your knees or with your legs crossed and set a timer for 2 minutes. Close your eyes, take a few deep breaths, and then open your eyes and maintain eye contact with your partner until the timer goes off, all in silence. Afterward, open up to your partner about any emotions that might be surfacing.

Try a New Hobby: Find something that you and your partner have not tried and are interested in and try it together. This will give you a new experience to look forward to and discuss after, and nurture bonding while you try it.

Plan Date Nights: Set out a day on a weekly or monthly basis to have date nights that you and your partner take turns in planning. Shake up what you are doing; maybe dinner, a yoga class, minigolf, or whatever suits your fancy.

It is one thing to know what goes into a healthy relationship and another to put it into practice. In the next chapter, you will discover how to effectively communicate with your partner.

Chapter 2:
30 Ways to Effectively Communicate

"Ultimately the bond of all companionship, whether in marriage or in friendship, is conversation."

— *Oscar Wilde*

Communication

Healthy communication is an important pillar of all relationships and is key to maintaining a long-lasting partnership. People are different. Your partner will not feel things in the same way you do and will have different expectations, priorities, and concerns. Being able to explain and discuss these with your partner will allow you to understand how the other person feels and help you to feel connected.

All relationships go through ups and downs, but with the right communication skills, individuals can learn how to effectively discuss their issues and resolve conflict.

How to Communicate

If you are upset about something or feel the need to otherwise bring up an issue with your partner, consider first how and what you are feeling. This might sound silly, but rushing into extensive talks with your partner before you have reflected on the emotions you are feeling and why you might be feeling them can be counterproductive. This is also not always the case – you might be feeling confused and overwhelmed and need a shoulder to lean on, in which case you should reach out to your partner to help you through your emotions.

- Set time aside without distractions to speak to your partner.

- Think about what you want to say and how you want to say it beforehand, and if possible, bring potential solutions if you are raising an issue.

- Use 'I' statements to discuss how you are feeling and what is affecting you, for example, "I feel upset when you forget to reply to my messages, and it makes me feel like you do not care," as opposed to "You are selfish and thoughtless for not replying to me." The latter will often make a person feel attacked and could lead them to act defensively.

- Accept responsibility for your feelings.

- Listen to your partner if they have anything to say without passing judgment.

In 'Nonviolent Communication,' psychologist Marshall Rosenberg developed an apt four-stage communication technique. They are as follows:

1. **Observations:** Initially, you begin by communicating your view observation of the situation without passing judgment, even if you do find yourself interpreting your partner's actions in some way. Say for example they never plan dates, and you find yourself planning all of your time together. You might bring this up by saying, "I have noticed that I have done most of the organization and planning for our dates recently on my own." You might feel like this is a result of them not caring enough about you, but avoid beginning the communication with this interpretation.

2. **Feelings:** Follow up your observation by telling your partner how this action makes you feel. Avoid attacking them, but use 'I' statements to show how you are directly affected, for example, "I am beginning to feel hurt as I feel like I am putting more effort into planning our quality time together."

3. **Needs:** Express your needs to your partner and show how you would like to be treated, and let them decide whether or not they consider this possible. For example, "I would like to feel cherished and to feel like you are putting effort into our

relationship."

4. **Requests:** Finally, conclude with requests that your partner could do to improve the situation. For example, "I would appreciate it if you organized a date night once a month." This is different from a demand. You are not insisting that your partner does as you say, but providing them with a potential solution to the issue.

Active Listening

Being able to listen is just as important as being able to communicate, and plays a big part in successful communication. It goes beyond simply listening to a person to hearing and understanding their emotions, reflecting on what they are trying to say and how they are feeling, and then trying to understand what they need and how you can support them. It is also a big part of being empathetic and showing that, despite being a whole different person to your partner who feels things differently and has different values, you are still open-minded to their perspective and feelings.

Constantly talking over each other, interrupting, firing rapid questions without waiting for a response, and being quick to judge a situation is a form of non-active listening, and often a barrier to successful communication. This you want to avoid, and instead consider some of the active listening techniques listed below:

- Engage fully with what your partner is saying and be present in the conversation (no interrupting or thinking about what is for dinner).
- Avoid distractions like your phone or your surroundings.
- Use eye contact, open body language, and encouraging gestures like nodding your head.
- Ask questions about what your partner is saying to show you are listening and you are interested, such as, "How did that make you feel?" or "Could you tell me more about that?" or "What might you have done differently?"

- Paraphrase what they have told you back to them to show you understood, for example, "It sounds like you are saying you are upset by what your co-worker said to you," or "So you are saying you do not like how much we are spending on rent?"
- Avoid jumping to conclusions or passing judgment, or trying to finish the speaker's sentences for them.

Improving Communication

Maybe communicating and listening do not come naturally to you, and that is okay. It is a skill; some have it naturally, and some have to work at it to improve. If you do feel like you sometimes struggle to listen, to get your point across, or if your partner has flagged your communication skills, there are many ways to improve your communication. Actively seeking to do so is the first step in improving your communication, and in many ways very brave as it can be difficult to accept that you are lacking in your communication skills.

If you are looking to improve your communication skills, consider the following questions. Answer them for yourself or share them with your partner and compare your responses.

Are there any areas of unresolved conflict in your relationship? Do you find yourselves arguing about the same things?

_____

_____

_____

_____

_____

_____

Is there anything your partner does while communicating (or not communicating) that upsets you?

_____

_____

_____

Are there areas where you communicate effectively with your partner, and you feel heard and understood?

_____

_____

_____

_____

Is there anything you avoid talking about? If so, why?

_____

_____

_____

_____

How would you like things to be different?

_____

_____

_____

_____

Communication Pitfalls

As you improve your communication, you might notice areas where you or your partner fall short. No one communicates perfectly (following the four-step approach), never getting emotional or lashing out at the other person. If we did, we would be very robotic. However, avoid engaging in the following behaviors when communicating as they can amplify emotions and prevent you from being able to fully engage with your partner.

- Premature judgment or accusations
- Attempting to manipulate the conversation or your partner for a certain outcome
- Showing a lack of empathy or concern for your partner's feelings
- Coming off as superior and above your partner, degrading their intelligence in doing so
- An unwillingness to compromise on issues
- Being unable to think outside the box or see things from your partner's perspective

Signs of Communication Breakdown

If you feel like you are no longer talking to your partner as much as you used to, or when you do speak, it is largely arguing, it might be a sign that you are experiencing a communication breakdown in your relationship. You might also feel like you are not being listened to, feel unable to listen to your partner's perspective, or that you are avoiding tough topics altogether. If this is the case, intervene early when possible. Speak to your partner about your concerns and try to navigate them together, and do not be afraid to involve a relationship therapist when necessary to help you through your issues.

30 Ways to Effectively Communicate With Your Partner

To effectively communicate with your partner, I have shared 30 ways below:

1. **Be an Engaged Listener:** This means paying close attention to what the other person is saying. Engaged listening involves not only hearing the words but also understanding the emotions and intentions behind them. To do this, you can use the active listening techniques mentioned earlier, such as asking questions or paraphrasing what they said back to them.

2. **Pay Attention to Body Language:** Body language can convey a lot of information that words alone cannot, so it is important to be aware of both your own and your partner's nonverbal cues. This includes things like eye contact, facial expressions, and posture. Paying attention to body language can help you understand the other person's emotions and level of engagement in the conversation.

3. **Keep Your Stress in Check:** It is important to find ways to manage your stress, such as meditation, mindfulness, breathwork, or exercise, so you can avoid letting your stress filter out into communication. This will help you stay calm and focused, and reduce the likelihood of misunderstandings or conflict.

4. **Consider What You Are Saying:** Reflect on what you want to say before bringing

up an important topic with your partner. Coming to a conversation with a clear idea of what you want to say can help you avoid misunderstandings and conflict, and build stronger relationships based on mutual understanding and respect.

5. **Stay Comfortable:** Being physically comfortable during a conversation can help you stay relaxed and focused. This means finding a comfortable position, away from potential distractions or things that could detract from the conversation.

6. **Limit Distractions:** This means giving the other person your full attention and avoiding distractions such as your phone or daydreaming, so you show that you are fully engaged.

7. **Make Eye Contact:** Making direct (appropriate) eye contact shows the other person that you are engaged and interested in the conversation.

8. **Use 'I' Statements:** 'I' statements focus on your feelings and experiences, rather than placing blame or criticism on the other person. This can help you express yourself more clearly and avoid making the other person feel defensive.

9. **Ask Open-Ended Questions:** Asking your partner open-ended questions shows that you are interested and engaged, and can prompt them to share more of their thoughts and feelings.

10. **Do Not Interrupt:** Interrupting or talking over your partner can undermine what they are saying and prevent effective communication. It is important to let the other person finish speaking before responding to show that you value their thoughts and opinions.

11. **Reflect on What Has Been Said:** Reflecting on what your partner is saying can help you better understand their perspective and show that you are listening. You can do this silently or ask questions to help you develop your understanding.

12. **Use Collaborative Language:** Collaborative language involves using words and phrases that promote teamwork and cooperation, and shows your partner that you are ready to work together, not apart. For example, "We can work through the solutions together."

13. **Keep the Communication Flowing:** Effective communication is a two-way street. It is important to both listen and respond and to keep the conversation flowing. Standing and staring at your partner in silence while they share a difficult conversation with you will likely make them feel uncomfortable. Avoid this by asking questions or providing feedback.

14. **Let Go of Blame:** Even if you are upset, avoid pointing fingers or suggesting your partner is to blame, as well as any accusatory language.

15. **Know and Accept That Your Partner May Have a Different View:** Your partner may have a different perspective or opinion than you do when it comes to big life changes or small ones. Acknowledge that your partner's views are just as valid as your own, and try to understand their perspective by actively listening to their point of view. This does not mean you have to agree with them, but by understanding where they are coming from, you will be better equipped to find a solution that works for both of you.

16. **Focus on What You Can Control:** Focus on what you can change, rather than what you cannot. It is important to remember that you cannot control your partner's

thoughts, feelings, or actions. Instead, focus on your behavior and how you can positively impact the relationship. If you are feeling frustrated or unhappy, identify what changes you can make to improve the situation. By focusing on what you can control, you will feel more empowered and less helpless.

17. **Avoid Unnecessary Conflict:** Conflict is inevitable in any relationship, but not all disagreements are worth fighting over. Pick your battles wisely and avoid unnecessary conflict. When disagreements do arise, try to remember that you love your partner, find common ground, and work toward a resolution that you are both happy with.

18. **Treat Your Partner as You Want to Be Treated:** Treat your partner with kindness, respect, and empathy, and consider how you might feel if you were on the receiving end of a verbal attack if you are tempted to personally lash out.

19. **Actions Are as Important as Words:** If you make a promise, say you will change, or say you will stop talking about something, you need to follow through with it. Failing to do so creates an environment of distrust and resentment.

20. **Ask Before Bringing Up Potentially Triggering Topics:** Some topics may be sensitive or triggering for your partner, and that is okay. If you do feel the need to raise something, ask your partner if they are okay with discussing the topic beforehand to show that you respect their boundaries.

21. **Do Not Be Sarcastic or Passive Aggressive:** Sarcasm and passive-aggressive behavior can be hurtful and damaging to a relationship. Instead, communicate your feelings directly and calmly, and avoid engaging in communication that might enflame a situation.

22. **Express Your Wants and Needs:** Your partner is not a mind reader, so it is up to you to communicate your desires. By expressing your wants and needs, you allow your partner to meet them and improve the relationship.

23. **Ask "What Do You Need From Me Right Now?"** Particularly if your partner raises an issue, this question shows that you are willing to support your partner, to learn and adapt, and to meet their needs.

24. **Know That You Are Going to Be Wrong Sometimes, and That Is OK:** No one is perfect, and everyone makes mistakes. It is important to accept when you are wrong and to apologize when necessary.

25. **Slow Down When Things Start to Escalate:** If you notice things start to get heated and conflicts start to escalate, it is important to take a step back and slow down. This can help you avoid saying or doing something you will regret later. Take a deep breath, count to ten, or take a break from the conversation to calm down rather than stoke the fire.

26. **Boost Your Partner's Self-Esteem:** Tell your partner they are sexy, that you appreciate their kindness, that you love how they show up for you, and that they are great at what they do. Making your partner feel good about themselves in a relationship means they feel confident and valued, it can improve the overall quality of your relationship.

27. **Hold Onto Your Values:** It is important to hold onto your values in a relationship because they define who you are as a person. By staying true to your values, you can maintain a sense of self-respect, integrity, and authenticity. It is also important to

communicate your values to your partner, so they understand what is important to you.

28. **While Also Being Open to Your Partner and Willing to Grow:** While holding onto your values is important, it is also important to recognize that change is a natural part of life. In a relationship, both partners may change, evolve, and grow together. It is important to be open-minded and flexible to change while staying true to your values.

29. **Be Tactful:** Tactfulness is the ability to communicate respectfully and sensitively. Being tactful involves being mindful of your tone, word choice, and timing when communicating with your partner, and respecting their emotions and boundaries.

30. **Accept When Your Partner Tells You "No":** Respecting your partner's boundaries is crucial in a healthy relationship. If your partner tells you "No" to something, it is important to accept their answer and not pressure or manipulate them into changing their mind. Doing so can damage trust and respect in the relationship.

Activities

Want to work on your communication skills? Try out the following exercises with your partner:

Twenty Questions

The name is self-explanatory. Think up twenty unique questions with your partner (or use the questions listed in Chapter 8), and discuss your answers to get a better insight into their dreams, values, and feelings. Below are some examples:

46

What was your first impression of me?

_____

_____

_____

_____

What is your happiest memory?

_____

_____

_____

_____

Where do you see yourself in five years?

_____

_____

_____

_____

What is your favorite date that we have been on?

_____

_____

_____

_____

Two Truths and a Lie

You probably played it with your friends, or at some point, but two truths and a lie can be a great way to get to know your partner and engage in listening and learning from each other. The premise is simple; think up two truths and a lie and try to swindle your partner into guessing that the lie is something you have experienced.

This or That?

A quickfire communication game can be great, especially earlier in your relationship when you want to know more about each other. For example:

Sweet or savory?

Morning or night?

Netflix and chill or fancy dinner?

Clubbing or staying in?

Cats or dogs?

Would You Rather?

A step up from the above, think of the weirdest scenarios you can think of and pose them to your partner. Have fun discussing each other's answers.

Would you rather be rich or happy?

_____

Would you rather speak every language or be able to speak to animals?

_____

Would you rather always be too hot or too cold?

_____

Would you rather continue your life or restart it?

_____

Would you rather be able to fly or read minds?

_____

Gratitude

Sometimes we forget to show the people we love how much we appreciate them. Set some time aside and think of three things that your partner has done for you that you appreciate, write them down, and consider how to thank them and show your appreciation.

For example, "I am so grateful that you got my favorite breakfast for me this morning. I was really happy when you remembered my order."

Listen and Draw

Sitting down with your partner with papers and pens, have one person verbally instruct on what the other should draw. One small circle, connected to a bigger oval by a rectangle. Four lines coming out of that rectangle. Now cover it in spots and add two lines off of the small circle. Have you drawn a giraffe? Well, me neither! This can still be a great way to work on your communication and teamwork, probably less so on your drawing skills.

Communicating with your partner is easy when times are good, but what about when things become more difficult? In the next chapter, you will be gaining some insight into how to work through conflict with your partner in a positive way.

Chapter 3:

How to Effectively Resolve Conflict

"Conflict can and should be handled constructively; when it is, relationships benefit. Conflict avoidance is *not* the hallmark of a good relationship. On the contrary, it is a symptom of serious problems and of poor communication."

— Harriet B. Braiker

The Importance of Respect, Even During Arguments

Conflict exists in all relationships, regardless of whether couples acknowledge it or not. People see the world differently and have different values and expectations, and it is normal to disagree with your partner in certain areas. However, when in conflict or communicating with your partner, it is most important that you maintain your respect for them and their personal opinions, and find a healthy approach to resolving disagreements appropriately.

Respect

A big part of healthy communication and conflict resolution is respect. This is a two-way street and goes for you and your partner. This means considering your partner an equal and not trying to show authority over them. Mutual respect also includes accepting your differences and honoring your partner's thoughts and feelings, even if you might disagree with them. You also have to work on having faith and trust in them and their decision-making. The trust side of things might take time to build up. Especially in an early relationship, or if you have been hurt before, trusting someone might be difficult, but with cohesive communication and ample respect, you will build this up gradually.

Mutual respect in a relationship looks like the following:

- Working on your communication by speaking honestly and being open about what you are feeling
- Actively listening
- Accepting your differences
- Compromising on issues
- Supporting each other through tough times
- Celebrating each other's successes
- Being kind, appreciative, and empathetic
- Respecting each other's boundaries
- Choosing not to speak in a degrading manner or attack your partner verbally

While you should respect your partner, you ideally also need to respect yourself. Self-respect is a big part of being able to respect others and maintain healthy relationships. It involves accepting yourself, even if you are conscious of your flaws, and embracing your individuality. It also extends to self-care and looking after your mind and body; whether this is nutrition, exercise, hobbies, meditation, or whatever makes you feel good about yourself.

Ways That You Can Show Respect to Your Partner

As mentioned earlier, respect plays a big role in healthy communication and conflict resolution. Below are some ways to show respect to your partner:

- Listen actively to your partner's needs, concerns, and desires.
- Act upon what you learn about these needs and concerns.
- Express acknowledgment, appreciation, and gratitude for what your partner does for you.
- Use humor carefully and playfully, without causing harm to your partner.

- Respect your partner's confidentiality and keep intimate details private.
- Avoid crossing the line from complaint to criticism.
- Refrain from using sarcasm and instead use gentle language.
- Address your partner directly instead of complaining to others.
- Communicate without impatience or irritability.
- Show compassion and forgiveness when your partner makes mistakes and reassure them that everyone can learn from their errors.

Common Causes of Relationship Conflict

Things that upset you or your partner and set you off will vary in every relationship. Nonetheless, here are some common causes to look out for, to help you avoid situations of conflict and to consider how you will respond without starting arguments if they do arise:

Jealousy and Possessiveness: This involves mistrust, tracking your every move, and disliking when you have your interests or want to see your friends.

Speaking in a Condescending Manner and Acting Superior: Criticizing your partner and acting superior to them, lashing out, and saying things that demean your partner's self-worth.

Unreliability: They say they will do one thing, or change, but never do, so you begin to grow resentful and do not believe what they say.

Lack of Emotion and Neglecting Your Relationship: They do not call or do not seem to have time for you, ignore your feelings, and do not show emotion or appreciation.

Unfaithfulness: This can extend from full-blown cheating to lying about their whereabouts or messaging someone they should not be.

Being Inconsiderate: This can include being inconsiderate in a home space, leaving dirty dishes out or failing to help with chores, to lacking consideration for your feelings.

Finances: If you share financial obligations, it is not uncommon that conflict might arise if someone is concerned about how much is being spent, or on what.

Intimacy: Particularly in marriage, conflict can arise over intimacy. Couples might find themselves at odds if one person has a higher sex drive, with the other feeling pressured or ashamed.

Conflict Resolution Tips

When you face conflicts with your partner, below are some tips that could help resolve them:

Find the Source of the Issue: Sometimes, you might find yourself arguing with your partner for no reason. This can be a product of unresolved issues bubbling up if they were not addressed at the time. Maybe your behavior is making your partner feel insecure, or vice versa. Maybe they are just so angry that you have not been making time for them, so leaving your socks on the floor on one occasion turns into World War III. Whatever the case, try and work with your partner to pinpoint what is causing the conflict so you can solve the root of the problem.

Establish and Maintain Your Boundaries: Even amid an argument, you should still treat your partner with respect and expect the same. Do not stoop to name-calling or harsh insults when addressing conflict, and call your partner out if this starts happening. Conflict resolution requires mutual respect on both sides.

Compromise and Work Together: Resolving conflict on your own is almost impossible. Working together and taking turns to 'give' where needed will help you stay on the same path in the long run. This also means not approaching it from the perspective of 'winning' or 'losing,' but rather collaborating so that everyone comes out the other side satisfied. Of course, stay true to your values. Some things are non-negotiable, but be ready to be flexible and compromise when needed.

Agree to Disagree: Even after butting heads with your partner or listening to one another make extensive and detailed explanations about why you feel a certain way, you might still not agree with one another. If this concerns a major life choice (think having children, or constant communication), and you cannot agree, you may well not be compatible. If however you can live and accept you both see an issue differently, try and accept this and move on without reviving the area of conflict, and know when to let an issue go.

Validate Each Other's Feelings: Following on from the above, while you might disagree or feel called out by something your partner brings up, it is important that you still acknowledge and validate how they are feeling. Reacting prematurely and telling your partner they are wrong, they are overreacting, or they are stupid for feeling a certain way will leave them feeling unheard and misunderstood. Instead, acknowledge how they are feeling, even if you think it is unwarranted or does not initially agree.

Revisit Your Feelings for One Another: Being in the middle of conflict can mean that you temporarily lose sight of how you value your partner, how much you love them, and how much they mean to you. When faced with what you might be viewing as an opponent across the battlefield, pause and try and remember the good memories you share - perhaps when you first met or a particularly nice memory - and how much you do value one another, which can help to reduce feelings of anger or resentment and help you to work together.

Reaffirm That You Love Your Partner: This might be difficult in the heat of the moment, but telling your partner, "I want you to know that I love you so much and you are more important to me than this issue," recenters your feelings for one another and reaffirms that you are teammates and partners working together to solve a problem.

When Appropriate, Use Humor to Deflect Conflict: Teasing your partner while they are opening up to you probably will not be proper, but they do say that laughter is the best medicine. When appropriate, try and lighten the mood with gentle and kind humor, but be sensitive and consider how this comes across.

Some arguments and areas of conflict cannot be sorted out between two people in a relationship, and you might need to involve a mediator. Seeking professional help from a couples therapist or counselor is not something to be ashamed of. A therapist can help you both improve your communication and conflict-resolving skills to avoid future issues and can be incredibly beneficial in the long run.

Be Empathetic, It Will Keep You in the Right Mindset

Empathy and sympathy; often confused. Sympathy tends to refer to pity or sorrow toward someone else's misfortune. Empathy generally means being open-minded and compassionate in trying to understand what someone else is feeling, even if you have not been through the same experience.

While past experience helps you be empathetic, it is not necessarily required. For example, if someone loses their job and goes bankrupt, you might respond:

With Sympathy: "I am sorry, that sucks."

With Empathy: First, imagine how you would feel if this happened to you. Maybe you also went through a bout of hardship as a child and can relate to that experience, or can otherwise imagine the difficulties that the person is going through if you cannot directly relate to the experience; "I am sorry to hear you lost your job. I imagine you must be going through an incredibly difficult time and feeling very frustrated."

Empathy is an incredibly important aspect of relationships, as you can deepen your relationship with your partner by being able to understand and reflect on how your partner is feeling. Through being empathetic, you work to overcome your differences with your partner by putting yourself in their shoes when it comes to understanding their emotional reactions. Empathy often works as a bridge between two people who see and respond to things differently; rather than arguing about these issues, with empathy, you begin to see the world from someone else's perspective, which helps you navigate challenges and overcome conflict.

Types of Empathy

Empathy generally comes in three different categories:

Cognitive: This follows the ability to consider and think about how others are feeling using your understanding and intellect. This helps often in seeing the broader picture and negotiating with different viewpoints.

Emotional: Being able to physically feel what another person is experiencing is generally categorized as emotional empathy. For example, finding yourself incredibly buoyant and happy when your friend or partner is in a good mood, or down and saddened if they are also low. This often helps most in relationships, but can also be overburdening if you are an extremely empathetic individual, as you can feel overwhelmed by the emotions of others.

Compassionate: In compassionate empathy, you consider and feel someone else's emotions, and feel moved to help them. It is usually a blend of cognitive and emotional empathy and also involves a desire to help and support.

For example, your partner comes home from work upset because they have not been chosen for a promotion they were initially promised.

Cognitive Empathy Response: "I can understand why you are angry; you were looking forward to that promotion."

Emotional Empathy Response: "That is so annoying! I know you were so looking forward to it and had your hopes up. I bet you feel so angry. I feel angry for you."

Compassionate Empathy Response: "I know you worked hard for that promotion, so I can understand why you would be so upset. Is there anything you might be able to do to bring this up at work or ensure you get a promotion next time around since you deserve it?"

Empathy Differences Between Genders

Studies show that females are in general stronger empathizers than males, particularly when it comes to cognitive empathy. This has been shown through numerous studies, most recently in a study conducted by Cambridge University in 2022 which involved participants from 57 countries. Of course, this does not immediately mean that your partner (if male) lacks total empathy, but is something to take into consideration if you do feel sometimes unheard.

A Lack of Empathy

Like communication, empathy comes naturally to some. To others, it takes time and practice to develop. A lack of empathy in you or your partner might present in the following signs:

Responding Inappropriately: You share a deep and dark secret or expose your vulnerability to your partner, and they respond by brushing it off, joking, or saying something sarcastic. Being unable to hear and support someone in need appropriately is a key sign of a lack of empathy.

Unaware of How Their Behavior or Responses Affect Others: Low empathy can result in someone acting selfishly, often unaware of how this might hurt or impact others.

They might even be aware of how this behavior is hurtful, but not feel overly remorseful about it.

Calling Others 'Too Sensitive': An inability to understand what other people are feeling can lead to an individual with low empathy lashing out and dismissing their emotions, calling them overly sensitive or saying that they are overreacting.

Inability to Connect to Other People's Experiences: Equally, a person with low empathy will have difficulty imagining themselves in the shoes of someone who has gone through something difficult. It has not happened to them and they cannot imagine what it would feel like to go through it, so they shut off and are unable to engage or support the person.

Being Hypercritical: When issues do arise or someone slips up, a person with low empathy cannot see the bigger picture and understand the reasons that might contribute to this issue.

Causes of Low Empathy

Low empathy can be caused by upbringing, genetics, or other life experiences. Certain mental conditions can lead to low empathy, including borderline personality disorder, autism, and narcissistic personality disorder. Equally, having low emotional intelligence can also lead to a lack of empathy, as can trauma, or periods of prolonged stress.

Tips for Cultivating Empathy Within Yourself

To cultivate empathy within yourself, consider the tips below:

Reflect on Your Own Emotions Through Mindfulness: Mindfulness is the practice of paying attention to the present moment, without judgment. By practicing mindfulness, you can become more aware of your own emotions and develop a greater understanding of how they affect your thoughts and actions.

Stop Judging Your Own Emotions as Negative: Many people judge their own emotions as either positive or negative and tend to suppress negative emotions like anger, fear, or sadness. However, by acknowledging and accepting all of your emotions, you can become more open and accepting of the emotions of others.

Imagine What Other People Are Feeling and Be Curious: Empathy involves being able to imagine what someone else is feeling and understanding their perspective. To cultivate empathy within yourself, try to imagine what others might be feeling in different situations. Ask open-ended questions to encourage others to share their feelings and experiences, which can help you develop a deeper understanding of their perspective.

Ask for Feedback: It can be helpful to ask for feedback from others about how they perceive you and your interactions with them. By listening to feedback, especially from your partner, you can gain a better understanding of how your actions and words affect them.

Get Out of Your Routine, Travel, and Be Open-Minded: Getting out of your routine, traveling to new places, and exposing yourself to different cultures and perspectives can help you develop empathy by broadening your worldview. By meeting people who have different experiences and backgrounds than your own, you can gain a better understanding of their perspective and develop a greater sense of empathy and compassion.

Practicing Empathy in Your Relationship

Whether or not you consider yourself an empathetic person, being conscious of how to respond to your partner, and if you think you are lacking in the department, working toward being more open and empathetic is incredibly important to maintaining a long-lasting relationship. To do so, try and employ the following:

Active Listening: As I have stressed before, one of the key components of empathy is being able to actively listen to others. This means giving your full attention to the person speaking, asking clarifying questions, and reflecting on what you have heard to ensure understanding.

Take the Time to Slow Down: It is easy to get caught up in the rush of daily life, but slowing down can help you become more attuned to the emotions and needs of your partner. Take time to reflect on your own emotions and experiences, and make equal space for your partner to share their thoughts and feelings.

Be Willing to Grow and Work on Yourself: Empathy is a skill that can be developed and improved over time and can evolve and grow with your relationship. This requires a willingness to be open and vulnerable, and challenging at times, but incredibly worthwhile in the long run.

Be Mindful of Your Partner: This means paying attention to their emotions, needs, and perspectives. It involves putting yourself in their shoes and being empathetic, compassionate, and respectful.

Be Willing to Work Through Past Trauma: Past trauma can affect our ability to empathize with others. If relevant, it is important to recognize and work through any past traumas or experiences that may be hindering your ability to connect with others on an emotional level or be mindful that your partner might also need extra support to work through their trauma. This may involve seeking therapy or other forms of support to help heal.

Acceptance

Acceptance is crucial for building healthy relationships both with your partner and with yourself. When you accept your partner for who they are and embrace their 'flaws' without pushing for imminent change, it creates a space of understanding and trust. Equally, accepting yourself promotes self-love and self-esteem, and means acknowledging your insecurities and shortcomings.

Flaws aside, some things you do need to work with your partner to improve, if you are experiencing issues in your relationship, for example with communication or timeliness, or other minor obstacles. Following this, acceptance does not mean complacency. It also includes knowing when to let go, when you have realized that something cannot be changed. For instance, if your partner does not want children, and you do. This can be discussed and communicated, but ultimately, you have to accept their decision and decide if your relationship is still worth continuing. Or, if they have a notorious temper. You can work together on this and try to improve things, but if you hit a roadblock, this is another area where you have to accept them the way that they are and either continue the relationship while acknowledging this or decide that you cannot change them and you are not compatible.

Acceptance in Relationships

When working on acceptance in your relationship, consider the following:

Honesty: Honesty is a crucial aspect of acceptance in relationships, and involves being truthful with yourself and your partner, as well as being open about your thoughts, feelings, and intentions.

Admitting Your Mistakes: If you mess up, acknowledge it. Admitting your mistakes is a key part of accepting responsibility, and shows that you are playing your part in the relationship.

Accepting That There Will Always Be Struggles: No relationship is perfect, and there will always be struggles and challenges. Accepting this reality can help build resilience and foster a sense of acceptance and understanding, and make you feel less stressed when conflict does arise.

Be Vulnerable, Even if It Scares You: Fear can be a major obstacle to acceptance in relationships. It is important to recognize and acknowledge your fears but also to challenge them and open yourself up to your partner.

Know Your Strengths: Knowing and relying on your strengths and abilities can help build confidence and foster a sense of self-acceptance, and help you feel safe and secure both in yourself and your relationship.

Be Open-Minded and Eager to Learn: Acceptance requires an open mind and a willingness to let go of previous biases. It means being open to different perspectives and ideas and being willing to learn and grow with your partner.

Set Goals and Work Toward Them: Goal setting is important, and making plans can help your relationship grow. This involves being proactive when issues do arise and working with your partner to make sure you are on the same run to achieve the things that matter most to you.

Fair Fighting Rules

When you do next end up in conflict with your partner, consider employing the following tactics:

Understand Your Feelings Before Starting an Argument: Take a moment to reflect on why you are feeling upset. Are you reacting to the situation at hand, or is there an underlying issue that is bothering you? If there is another issue at the core of your conflict, how might you bring that up?

Stick to One Topic at a Time: Avoid bringing up a flood of bottled-up anger and resentment. Focusing on one specific issue helps keep the conversation on track and increases the chances of resolving it.

Avoid Degrading Language and Personal Attacks: These types of comments can escalate the argument and hurt your partner's feelings and can make conflict far harder to resolve.

Express Your Feelings With 'I' Statements: Use 'I' statements to communicate how you feel without accusing or blaming your partner.

Practice Active Listening: Take turns speaking and give your full attention to your partner, as this will help you both feel heard and understood.

Avoid Stonewalling and Yelling: Shutting down, going mute, giving your partner the silent treatment, or yelling and blowing up can be damaging to the relationship and prevent the problem from being resolved.

Take a Time-Out if the Discussion Becomes Too Heated: Sometimes it is necessary to step away and cool down before continuing the conversation. This can allow you both to calm down and refocus on the issue at hand.

Attempt to Come to a Compromise or Understanding: It might not be the perfect solution, but striving for a mutual understanding can help improve the relationship and prevent future arguments.

Activities

Getting good at conflict resolution takes practice and varies in each relationship. Try out some of the following questions and exercises to assess your current approach and how you might improve upon it.

How Do I Respond to Conflict?

Consider your past arguments and try and reflect on what went right, what went wrong, and what you might have done differently. You can work with your partner on this or do it alone.

Are there any unresolved arguments or areas of conflict that you think need addressing?

_____

_____

_____

When in conflict with your partner, did you do or say anything that you regret, that you feel worsened your ability to resolve the situation?

_____

_____

_____

Is there anything your partner said or did that you feel made things worse?

_____

_____

_____

_____

Can you think of any solutions to past conflicts? (No wrong answers, and do not judge your partner on theirs if you are working together).

_____

_____

_____

Discuss the solutions if working with your partner, and try to agree on one. How might you work toward achieving this?

_____

_____

_____

Remove Relationship Disturbances

Arguing about the same things? If these can be easily removed, consider sitting down with your partner and trying to identify them. Ask yourselves the following questions:

What are we disagreeing/arguing over?

_____

_____

_____

How do I react?

_____

_____

_____

_____

How do you react?

_____

_____

_____

_____

How might we be able to remove these disturbances or work through these issues?

_____

_____

_____

_____

_____

Let Us Both Win

It is easy to get caught up in waging a war against your partner and feeling superior if you come out on top. However, try to move past that mentality and find a mindset where you are asking yourself not "How do I get what I want?" but instead, "How do we both get what we want?"

Try and discuss this with your partner and work toward a vision where you work alongside each other to compromise and find satisfaction. To do so, consider the following when analyzing your arguments:

What caused the conflict?

_____

_____

_____

_____

What is each person's idea of a 'win' or an ideal outcome?

_____

_____

_____

_____

How can we combine these to find an outcome where we are both happy?

_____

_____

_____

Couple Check-Ins

Even if you are not in the middle of an argument, consider setting regular time aside to check in with your partner. This way, you can source any small issues as they arise and avoid letting them grow into huge areas of conflict if not spoken about.

Ask yourselves the following:

What are we doing well in our relationship that we could try to do more of?

_____

_____

_____

_____

_____

_____

_____

What is not working in our relationship that we could improve on?

_____

_____

_____

_____

Are there any things we could start doing that would benefit us?

_____

_____

_____

_____

Is there anything that is causing recurrent issues that we need to stop doing?

_____

_____

_____

_____

Sometimes it is not what you necessarily say and how you say it, but how your personalities clash. In the next chapter, you will discover how temperament can impact a relationship.

Chapter 4:

Temperament and How It Affects Relationships

"The most important kind of freedom is to be what you really are. You trade in your reality for a role. You trade in your sense for an act. You give up your ability to feel, and in exchange, put on a mask. There can't be any large-scale revolution until there's a personal revolution, on an individual level. It's got to happen inside first."

– Jim Morrison

How Personalities Can Affect Relationships

I f everyone had the same personality, life would be boring. It is also often true that people with different personalities, different mannerisms, traits, and characteristics tend to attract one another. After all, seeing someone else exhibiting traits you perhaps lack, that you appreciate and feel inspired by, can often work to bring out the best version of yourself. However, personality differences can also be a great inhibitor to successful relationships. What you once thought was an attractive trait in your partner can grow to be an element that you actively dislike. It is therefore important to know and understand yourself and your partner when it comes to aligning yourself for a successful relationship.

What makes up your personality can stretch to all manners of things. It can involve your values and morals, your feelings (whether you might consider yourself overly sensitive, or lacking empathy). Whether you are chatty and the life of the party, or more of an introvert who likes to skirt around corners. Whether you are passionate and driven, or seek a happy and smooth life. Your personality affects your thinking and behavior, and also how you are perceived by others, so understanding its implications is key to positioning yourself with your partner.

Personality Types

Studies have worked hard to organize different personality types into various categories. Amongst them, and perhaps the most typical model organizes personalities into the following:

- **Type A**: Ambitious, organized, competitive, and passionate
- **Type B**: Friendly, relaxed, dreamer, and charismatic
- **Type C**: Creative, independent, less social, and dependable
- **Type D**: Caring, shy, anxious, and often self-isolating

Myer-Briggs Personality Test: Another common personality categorization formula is the Myer-Briggs Type Indicator (MBTI), based on Jungian theories of personalization. This involves combining the below four divisions of personality types to form a broader category of 16 different personality types.

- **Extraversion (E) or Introversion (I):** Extraverts gain energy from external stimulation and tend to be outgoing, sociable, and expressive. Introverts, on the other hand, gain energy from within and prefer quieter, more reflective environments. They are often more reserved and introspective.

- **Sensing (S) or Intuition (N):** Sensing types rely on their five senses and prefer concrete, factual information. They pay attention to details and are realistic. Intuitive types focus on patterns and possibilities. They are imaginative and rely more on intuition and gut feelings.

- **Thinking (T) or Feeling (F):** Thinking types make decisions based on logic and analysis. They value fairness and consistency. Feeling types, by comparison, make decisions based on their values and morals and consider the impact on others. They prioritize empathy and emotional considerations.

- **Judging (J) or Perceiving (P):** Judging types prefer structure, organization, and planning. Perceiving types are more flexible, adaptable, and open-minded. They prefer spontaneity and unpredictability in life.

Combining these four divisions, the MBTI identifies a wider category of 16 different personality types composed by four-letter codes, for example, INFJ (Introversion, Intuition, Feeling, Judging) which would mean an individual is largely organized, insightful, self-aware, and able to compose their judgments.

How Is Personality Developed?

Nature and nurture – you have probably heard it before. What comes to constitute an individual's personality is often a combination of the following elements:

Genetics: Genetic factors play a role in shaping personality traits. Certain traits may be inherited, such as temperament and predispositions to certain behaviors or tendencies.

Upbringing: The environment we grow up in and our upbringing as a child has a huge impact on how we conduct ourselves as adults. This includes family dynamics, cultural expectations, and socio-economic factors, also extending to relationships with parents and siblings; all of which impact how we see the world.

Socialization: We learn social norms, values, and expectations through interacting with the world around us. This occurs with figures such as teachers, mentors, and other social influences, perhaps from popular media. Through interacting with others and watching them interact, we come to form our behavior based on these influences.

Life Experiences: Personal experiences and events also contribute to personality development. This includes both the good and the bad; extreme trauma can have life-long impacts on our personality. Equally, achievements can instill in us confidence and passion. These form a large portion of how we approach resilience and how we learn to cope with the challenges we face, and how we interact with those around us.

Self-Awareness: The ability to reflect on oneself and conduct introspection into how one behaves also allows for growth and the awareness of your personality. Being aware of your strengths and weaknesses, as well as your passions and dislikes, also contributes to the formulation of your wider personality.

How Does Personality Affect Mental Health?

It is important to note that while personality traits can impact a person's mental health, they are often not the sole factor behind any changes or the impact on well-being. Additional factors such as genetics, social circle, or environment can contribute to any issues. Nonetheless, the following personality traits can impact mental health:

Extraversion Versus Introversion: Extroverts tend to enjoy socializing more and develop supportive social circles, which can lead to better mental health outcomes. Introverts may feel self-sufficient and more comfortable alone and might need self-care to prevent feelings of being overwhelmed.

Neuroticism: Neuroticism has been linked with an increase in mental health issues such as anxiety and depression, particularly if an individual is prone to becoming overwhelmed and stressed.

Thinking Versus Feeling: Thinking types may prioritize logic and rationality, potentially suppressing emotions. Feeling types may prioritize empathy and harmony but can experience emotional sensitivity or difficulties setting boundaries and thus experience heightened anxiety.

Conscientiousness: Being able to plan and organize yourself can often lead to being able to take care of your body by exercising, eating well, and generally taking a responsible approach to life – which are all conducive to better mental health and well-being.

Open-Mindedness: Being open-minded and approaching the world with open eyes can often lead to better mental health and well-being compared to individuals who shirk new experiences and refrain from trying new things or learning from the perspective of others.

How Personality Can Affect Relationships

As I have mentioned earlier, opposites often attract – though this is not always the case. Some couples feel drawn to someone they consider their equal. You might hear a couple thrilled to have their equal counterpart in the opposite gender, as you might hear of a successful and contented couple enjoying how their personality differences interact.

Communication: Different personality types have different communication styles, which can impact how individuals can communicate and express their feelings, how they listen, and how they understand. Extraverts may be more outgoing and willing to share while introverts may prefer more thoughtful conversations or be less inclined to open up. These differences can sometimes lead to misunderstandings or challenges in effective communication in relationships.

Conflict Resolution: Some people may prefer direct and assertive communication and be unafraid of tackling tough topics aggressively or directly, while others may prefer a more harmonious and cooperative approach or to avoid conflict altogether.

Emotional Expression: Those who are open in sharing their feelings might struggle with a partner who is more reserved or finds it challenging to articulate their emotions.

Social Preferences: Personality traits can also influence social preferences and needs within relationships. A partner who enjoys quiet time alone might struggle alongside a partner who thrives in large social gatherings and enjoys a wide circle of friends.

Relationship Expectations: Some people may value independence in their relationship, while others may prioritize emotional connection and support, and desire a more codependent life, which can lead to a contradiction in how this couple aligns themselves in their life together.

Personality Disorders: Individuals with certain personality disorders might struggle more so when it comes to forming healthy and long-lasting relationships. This should never be taken as a complete hindrance from engaging in these relationships or believing that they can become fruitful; with correct therapeutic support, individuals with personality disorders can often also make wonderful lifelong partners. However, being aware of the disorders and their limitations is also key.

- Borderline Personality Disorder (BPD) may struggle with extreme highs and lows, black-and-white thinking, unstable self-esteem, a fear of abandonment, and otherwise struggle to maintain long-term relationships.

- Narcissistic Personality Disorder (NPD) can mean that individuals have an inflated sense of self-worth and require constant praise. This can lead to them acting selfishly in relationships, prioritizing their own needs, and at times manipulating their partner.

- Depressed individuals can also suffer from self-worth issues and a fear of abandonment, making them dependent on their partner or even pushing them away as a form of self-sabotage.

Personality disorders extend far beyond those mentioned, but it is worth opening up to your partner if you or they experience a disorder. Working together where possible will often lead to a higher chance of success and the ability to work out how to navigate challenges together; employing a therapist or mental health professional where possible.

How Personality Predicts Relationship Longevity

While personality traits can be gradually changed and adapted, large changes later in life are often not possible. Therefore, choosing someone aligned with your values is key to the longevity of your relationship.

Neuroticism above all is perhaps the highest indicator of a relationship that will experience difficulties down the line, while for couples looking for an emotionally-stable and long-lasting relationship, finding a partner who is not similar to them in every way, but is instead kind, agreeable, self-aware and conscientious is often the most indicative of the success of a relationship.

Attachment

The bond that you form with your partner is key to how you both interact and how you continue to emotionally connect and align yourselves as an enduring team.

Attachment is formed at an early age, generally between primary caregivers and infants. These early attachments are often conducive to how we develop relationships with our romantic partners and how we approach intimacy.

A turbulent and unsafe relationship with a parent or primary caregiver where you lacked attention or interaction from your parents may lead to fearfulness and fear of abandonment with your partner in later life and an insecure and anxious attachment style while watching your parents engage in a healthy and happy relationship can lead to you exemplifying these characteristics in your own life and being secure in your relationships. Nonetheless, whatever your infant relationships may have looked like, these do not have to mean a complete breakdown or the inability to connect as an adult. Knowing your attachment style and how you connect is often critical knowledge to expanding your relationships as an adult.

Different Attachment Styles

The different attachment styles are generally categorized as follows:

1. **Secure Attachment Style**
   - Individuals with a secure attachment style have positive self-esteem and are often trusting and welcoming.
   - They are comfortable with intimacy and embrace close and healthy relationships.
   - They trust their partners and have confidence in their ability to meet their partner's emotional needs.
   - They have effective communication skills and can express their needs and emotions clearly, and can listen effectively to what their partner desires.
   - They are generally able to maintain and respect healthy boundaries and can resolve conflict.
   - They are not overly worried about abandonment or rejection, nor plagued with insecurity.

2. **Avoidant Attachment Style**
   - They value independence, self-reliance, and personal space.

- They often have strong self-worth but feel like they do not need the involvement of an outside partner.
- They tend to avoid emotional intimacy and may have difficulties opening up emotionally.
- They may have commitment issues.
- They may struggle with expressing their emotions and may be dismissive or emotionally distant in relationships; avoiding communication or heavy topics.

3. Anxious Attachment Style

- Individuals with an anxious attachment style often have a negative view of themselves.
- They desire close and intimate relationships but have a fear of abandonment or rejection.
- They seek reassurance, validation, and constant contact from their partners, which can often push the other person away.
- They may appear clingy or needy.
- They may have difficulties with trust and may be sensitive to signs of rejection.
- They may experience heightened emotional highs and lows in relationships and may be prone to jealousy or possessiveness.

4. Fearful-Avoidant Attachment Style

- Individuals with a fearful-avoidant attachment style have negative views of both themselves and others.
- They desire close relationships but may struggle with trust and have a fear of getting hurt, thus choosing not to engage out of fear of being hurt.

- They may have difficulties managing their emotions and may experience internal conflicts in relationships; often riding between highs and lows in how they engage with their partners.

Cultivating a More Secure Attachment Style

Not all people can enter into relationships fully capable of opening their hearts and trusting someone else with ease. Due to a plethora of factors, people develop anxious or avoidant attachment styles and can struggle to build and maintain successful relationships owing to the struggles these attachment styles bring. However, once you have determined your attachment style, even if you are now realizing you are perhaps more anxious or avoidant than you thought, there is plenty that can be done to improve how you form relationships, which will be advantageous to forming and maintaining relationships throughout your life – not just with your partner.

Reflect on and Define Your Attachment Style: Take time to try and work out what your attachment style is. Understand how your life experiences have shaped your beliefs and behaviors in relationships, and examine any previous patterns or behaviors you have been through in past relationships.

Work on Self-Awareness: Remain aware of your own emotions and feelings, your requirements, and your triggers in relationships. Recognize any patterns of insecure attachment or if you tend to push people away to understand how they may be impacting your current relationships.

Work on How You Communicate and Open Up: Effective communication is vital for building a secure attachment. As I have stressed throughout this workbook, practice active listening, empathy, and expressing your needs and emotions clearly and assertively. It is not always easy, but opening up encourages honest communication with your partner and helps to ease insecurity and build trust.

Build on Trusting People: Building trust is essential for secure attachments. This can be immensely difficult for those with anxious or avoidant attachment styles, but work on being reliable and consistent in your words and actions. Follow through on your commitments and your words, and be present for your partner in the good times and the bad.

Be Vulnerable: Particularly if you have built up a wall around your emotions and your heart, opening up can be difficult. However, vulnerability is the key to love, even if it makes you more susceptible to getting hurt. A life shut away from the world, although it may seem safer, is an incredibly lonely journey. Thus, work on fostering a safe and supportive space for emotional vulnerability. Share your thoughts, feelings, and fears with your partner, and encourage them to do the same. Equally, show empathy, validation, and support when your partner shares their emotions.

Construct Healthy Boundaries: Establish and maintain healthy boundaries in your relationships, particularly if you have an anxious attachment style and tend to bend to your partner's every need or push yourself beyond your comforts to make them happy. Remain aware of your partner's boundaries and work on respecting each other's limits.

Be Kind to Yourself and Incorporate Self-Care: Healing from an anxious or avoidant attachment style requires a lot of self-love. It is a long and arduous journey, but incredibly worth it in the long run. Pushing yourself beyond your comfort zone can be challenging at times, so remember to be kind to yourself and your emotions, and continue looking after your own emotional and physical needs.

Seek Professional Help if Needed: Working through a particularly challenging attachment style can be difficult on your own. If you find yourself unable to move forwards successfully, perhaps due to past trauma or other experiences, or you find that the way you relate to others is significantly impacting your relationships, consider seeking assistance from a therapist. Professionals can provide valuable insight and help you work through any underlying issues, helping you to move forwards and build healthy and trusting partnerships.

What to Do if Your Personality Clashes With Your Partner

Different does not mean better or worse. It just means finding ways that work for you and your partner and navigating a method that works for both of you. This can mean working on your communication skills and active listening, your conflict resolution, discussing your expectations and finding a compromise on each side to find a situation in which both parties find solace in the outcome. In terms of attachment styles, this means also being aware of your partner's attachment style, and how you can best support them. For someone with an insecure attachment style, this means learning how to reassure them and give them support. For an avoidant, knowing when to give them space. Communicating openly and without judgment is often the best strategy for getting you and your partner on the same page in your relationship.

Different Personality Clashes and How to Navigate Them

For all of the differences mentioned above, it is not unlikely that you might find yourself clashing with your partner. When this happens, it is important to be aware of the clash and be ready to face it head-on. Common personality conflicts generally happen in one of the following scenarios:

Introversion Versus Extroversion: While an introverted individual might enjoy the life and enthusiasm an extroverted partner brings, they may also feel at times overwhelmed or unwilling to socialize to their degree. If you do experience conflict between your levels of engagement with the world with your partner, try to find a middle ground. Be conscious of your partner's boundaries and know when to moderate yourself to make them feel comfortable as an extrovert, and try to consciously push yourself outside of your comfort zone when necessary to accommodate a more extroverted partner.

For example, your partner loves socializing and spending late nights with friends, yet you feel often overwhelmed. Set certain time limits and come to an understanding whereby you are both happy in your time spent together in the presence of others, or work to spend time on your interests separately.

Different Values and Morals: One individual might have more liberal views and be more open-minded, while the other is more conservative. Everyone is entitled to their view, and navigating this requires being respectful and mindful of your partner's wishes, and finding a compromise where you both grow and are flexible to the morals of the other, yet do not push each other to an unnecessary degree.

For example, your partner comments on your outfit of choice. It is too tight, too short. Everyone is in charge of their own decisions and appearance, but this requires an understanding on both parts, whereby you respect your partner's wishes but also reinforce the fact that you are your individual and they must work to accept and trust you for that fact.

Work Ethic: Your partner works hard and diligently, and prioritizes success, leaving you feeling left out and set aside (or vice versa). Communicating your goals and passions and working to find an aligned drive is key to discovering the necessary balance for relationship longevity.

For example, you are working incredibly hard on a new and important project, and your partner begins to feel left out. Be mindful of this, communicate how important the opportunity is to you, but work to set time aside to remind your partner that they are a priority in your life.

Political or Religious Views: Political or religious view clashes can be a divisive point of conflict in relationships. Being mindful and kind is always necessary to handle finding a life in which you can accommodate one another's beliefs and views and continue to live in harmony, in a way that incorporates both of your beliefs.

For example, you find yourself disagreeing with your partner over a sensitive issue, perhaps in the news or regarding moral values. Communicate, explain, and discuss your beliefs. Be open-minded to how your partner was raised and accept that you have your own set of beliefs and that you must learn to tolerate differences in faith or political alignment.

Treatment of Others: Perhaps your partner is a selfless and kind individual, who volunteers and donates to charities, or perhaps you are that individual. A contrast in how you treat others in a relationship can lead to conflict, which communication and understanding can help to soften. Relationships require a huge deal of willingness to grow and learn, and only by discussing these topics and working together can you work to overcome your communal understanding of compassion and understanding.

For example, you are overly conscious that your partner ignores waiters or waitresses and feel uncomfortable with this lack of appreciation. Communicating this concern helps you both work on your compassion and appreciation for those around you.

Thinkers Versus Feelers

Another term used to differentiate differences in personalities when it comes to relationships is 'thinkers' versus 'feelers.' Of course, we tend not to fall concretely into either category but are instead an amalgamation of both.

Thinkers tend to rely on logistics, analyzing situations when making decisions, and understanding their emotions. They prioritize facts, rationality, and consistency. They may appear more detached or analytical in their approach to relationships and may struggle with understanding or expressing emotions, often taking things at face value and struggling to read into the hidden meaning behind their partner's words.

Feelers, on the other hand, place a greater emphasis on emotions and feelings when making decisions and understanding their emotions. They prioritize empathy, harmony, and the impact of their actions on others. They may appear more sensitive and vigilant of the emotions of those around them.

Conflict can arise in a partnership between a thinker and feeler for a multitude of reasons, such as emotional expression and communication, how they approach conflict resolution, and understanding one another's emotional needs. For example, a feeler may say "I am fine," while internally wounded and hurt by something the thinker has done or said, which will be met by a lack of empathy or willingness to explore the situation more. Thinkers may also lack the same degree of emotional awareness feelers experience, making it difficult for them to comprehend or support their partner in this.

In a relationship where one party may be considered a 'thinker' and the other a 'feeler,' the best mode of working together to find harmony is open-mindedness and willingness to work to understand the perspective of the other. A 'thinker' should work on their emotional intelligence and empathy, while a 'feeler' should work on their ability to follow the logistical reasoning and formulaic approach their partner sees the world. Maintaining mutual respect, working on communication and active listening, and remaining empathetic throughout will help combat these issues and allow a couple to grow together.

Activities

If you find yourself navigating personality clashes, try out some of the following activities to try and help strengthen your connection and expose yourself to your partner's way of thinking:

Try Out Your Partner's Hobbies and Ask Them to Try Yours

It is easy to turn your head when your partner mentions golf, tennis, or drawing, and say, "God, no, that sounds so boring. I do not want to." However, ask your partner what they enjoy and embrace the opportunity to experience something that they love with them. This will show them your willingness to see their way of life and provide you with an opportunity to share mutual interests. Do also allow each other time apart and respect your interests when appropriate. Forcing yourself into your partner's weekly tennis game with their friends is unlikely to be beneficial.

What hobbies does my partner enjoy, that we have not yet tried together?

_____

_____

_____

_____

_____

Is there an experience or an activity that we both have discussed but not yet tried?

_____

_____

_____

_____

_____

What are your interests or hobbies that you would like your partner to try out?

_____

_____

_____

Take Turns Interviewing Each Other

This might sound dull, but it is not a job interview. Try digging deep into your partner's childhood, their thoughts on life, religion, and all other big topics. Be open-minded and encourage sharing, kindness, and healthy debate. This will foster an environment of open-mindedness and teach you more about how you both view certain aspects of life.

What are your future dreams?

_____

_____

_____

What do you think happens after life?

_____

_____

_____

What are your favorite childhood memories?

_____

_____

_____

_____

Schedule a Love-Language-Themed Date

Date nights should be a regular on the cards, but when doing so, try to alternate the focus between you and your partner, and your interests. If your partner loves spending quality time, work on a no-distraction bonding activity. If you or they love words or affirmation, work on a date where you push yourself to reassure them and voice your appreciation. Maintain an awareness of how you can best show your love and respect to work through clashes and show a willingness to accommodate one another.

Spend Time Apart

It might sound scary, or even counterproductive, but particularly for introverted/extroverted partnerships, scheduling time apart can help you both recharge and return to your relationship refreshed. The distance can often make the heart grow fonder!

Oftentimes conflict occurs and it is a one-time situation. However, it is not uncommon to be rehashing the same arguments over and over again. In these situations, you have likely developed an unhealthy relationship pattern. In the next chapter, you will discover how to identify relationship patterns and alter them when they are unhealthy.

Creating Connections Together

Halfway through this workbook, you are likely discovering new insights into your relationship. You are exploring ways to improve communication, deepen trust, and heighten intimacy. By now, you have started viewing your relationship through a fresh lens, seeing patterns and potential for growth in a new light. Just like you, many other individuals and couples are on similar paths, grappling with their relationship dynamics. They may be feeling confused, misunderstood, or alone, yearning for resources to help them navigate their unique relationship challenges. This is where your experience can provide valuable guidance. By sharing your honest thoughts about this workbook, you have the opportunity to provide reassurance and support to those on similar journeys.

Scan to leave a review !

Leaving a review on Amazon about your experiences so far, the changes you have observed, and the tools you have found useful does not just benefit you; it becomes a guiding light for others. Your review can help those feeling lost or overwhelmed in their relationships, showing them that they are not alone and pointing them toward resources that might resonate with them. Whether your experiences have been positive, or you have encountered challenges along the way, your feedback matters. It is more than just a review; it is an act of community support, a personal testimony, and a gesture of goodwill to others in need.

I appreciate your time and your willingness to share your thoughts. All feedback, be it positive or negative, is invaluable. Together, we can foster a community of understanding and support, encouraging healthier and happier relationships for all.

Sincerely,

Chloe Slater

Chapter 5:

Identifying and Altering Relationship Patterns

"We accept the love we think we deserve."

— Stephen Chbosky, The Perks of Being a Wallflower

What Are Relationship Patterns?

As we have explored, different individuals are often attracted to one another when it comes to romantic relationships. Additionally, individuals have different attachment styles and temperaments, all of which are built on the foundations of how our parents raised us, and the life experiences we went through. As creatures of habit, we tend to continue relying on our behaviors and repeating them throughout life. This also applies to how we interact with our partners; different people with different behaviors and expectations forming a relationship and coexistence can find themselves repeating certain interactions.

Identifying your relationship patterns requires a great degree of self-awareness. It can also be incredibly humbling to realize that one of your characteristics is causing the repeat of a certain relationship pattern that may be causing conflict between you and your partner. However, working on introspection and analyzing your relationship patterns and what they might be derived from is an exceptionally useful way to help you align your values and synchronize yourselves in your partnership.

What Do Unhealthy Relationship Patterns Look Like?

You want to be in constant contact with your partner, want to be able to track their movements and be texting throughout the day, yet your partner is less engaged with constant communication and this continually surfaces as an issue.

You are a big saver and are frugal with your money, but your partner continues to buy expensive items, fancy dinners, and lavish holidays and causing repeat conflict over the need to save versus the need to spend.

You love talking about the future — your big house, your future pets, and what you will call your children — but your partner shuts down at the mention of the future and causes resentment in their unwillingness to dream with you.

Relationship Pattern Labels

Introvert Versus Extrovert: A relationship pattern might emerge between one partner who desires alone time and needs to recharge away from socialization and their partner, while the other thrives from constant emotional connection and socialization.

Emotional Versus Logical: One partner is led by their heart and their emotions, while the other approaches situations based on facts and rationality.

Exaggeration Versus Understating: When a situation arises, one partner tends to stress and catastrophize. They might even jump to ultimatums. In contrast, the other partner downplays the conflict and minimizes their severity.

Finances: People have different spending habits. One big spender can lead to a great deal of conflict in a relationship with someone frugal.

Control Versus Freedom: Knowing where your partner is at all times, and wanting constant updates and reassurance can be ill-met by someone who wants the independence of living their own life daily.

Dreaming Versus Realism: Big dreams and prophesizing for the future can lead to repeat issues and conflict in the presence of someone who would prefer to focus on the present.

Teacher Versus Student: One partner might want to educate the other; broaden their mind, and teach them new ideas or new relationship aspects. The other partner might be unwilling to engage or learn from these teachings.

Routine Versus Spontaneity: A partner who loves adventuring, late nights, new experiences, and other spontaneous activities might find themselves in repeat conflict with someone who enjoys a consistent routine.

Co-Dependency*: Co-dependency can be a common yet unhealthy relationship pattern, whereby one individual relies excessively on their partner to bolster their self-worth and identity. This individual might feel lost and unable to function without the support of their partner, which can lead to an imbalance of power and an overreliance on the supporting partner. Co-dependency generally stems from low self-esteem and fears of abandonment stemming from childhood, leading them to always prioritize the needs of their partner over their own out of fear of being abandoned or rejected.

How Are Relationship Patterns Formed?

In the same way that our attachment styles are formed, the contributors behind relationship patterns delve back to childhood. The relationships we have with our parents and how much care and appreciation we received can determine the relationships we seek out as adults. The relationships our parents had with one another can also determine what we seek out as adults. For example, having a calm and quiet father figure might lead someone to seek out an individual with the same characteristics for their relationship, as they recognize this as their earliest experience of stable love. Having an emotional and turbulent mother figure can also lead individuals to seek out unpredictable and passionate figures in later life, having grown up under the influence of such a person.

How Can I Identify My Relationship Patterns?

Inner work is not easy by any means but is greatly beneficial to putting an end to relationship patterns that can sabotage your partnership. It requires a great deal of self-reflection; first at the relationship pattern that is occurring, and then at yourself. It also often means shifting the blame away from your partner. Perhaps they are not meeting your communication expectations and perhaps this is something that they too need to work on, but examining your need for constant reassurance and any fearfulness that might have caused this will help greatly in working through your issues. This is also not a solo project. Working with your partner to both identify your behaviors and the patterns that they cause is key to moving forwards in tandem toward a relationship that is mutual, loving, and built on self-awareness and respect.

Why Do We Repeat Destructive Patterns?

It might seem at times illogical, but children of alcoholics often end up marrying alcoholics. Children who grew up in abusive households often end up either on the receiving end or as perpetrators of abuse. However, returning to Chbosky's quote, "We accept the love we think we deserve."

We Repeat What We Know: Even if these behaviors cause us hurt and pain, humans tend to repeat them as they are familiar, and with familiarity comes a certain sense of comfort.

We Repeat Behaviors in an Attempt to Overcome Them: If you felt unacknowledged and unloved as a child, you might seek out a partner who appears equally cold and unloving. On an unconscious level, you might think that you can change them, and in the process heal from the trauma you experienced in your childhood rejection, thus taking control of your rejection. However, the outcome is often not as intended and leads to a repeat of feeling rejected and unloved.

We Believe We Deserve to Suffer: Growing up in a household where you were abused, neglected, lacked attention, or experienced other forms of trauma can lead to immense negative effects on self-esteem. Thus, as adults, we internalize that blame and think ourselves unworthy of healthy and reassuring love. We might think, "Yes, my partner fails to support me and does not connect with me on an emotional level – but, having been told that I am unworthy and stupid and unattractive, do I deserve any better?"

Signs of Unhealthy Relationship Patterns

Below are some questions to pose yourself regarding your relationship, to assess if you are experiencing any repeated unhealthy patterns in how you view your partner and feel in their presence.

1. *Do you find it difficult to trust your partner or constantly feel suspicious?*
2. *Are you experiencing excessive jealousy or possessiveness in your relationship?*
3. *Do you and your partner frequently engage in arguments and conflicts that escalate quickly and are blown out of proportion?*
4. *Does your partner exhibit controlling behavior or try to isolate you from friends and family?*
5. *Have you experienced any form of verbal or physical abuse from your partner?*
6. *Does your partner use disrespectful or demeaning language towards you?*
7. *Do you feel like your feelings and opinions are ignored or dismissed by your partner?*
8. *Have you noticed any patterns of emotional manipulation or guilt-tripping in your relationship?*
9. *Is there a lack of open and effective communication between you and your partner?*

10. *Do you regularly argue about spending?*

11. *Is there a noticeable power imbalance in your relationship, with one partner making most of the decisions?*

12. *Do you feel unsupported in pursuing your goals and aspirations by your partner?*

13. *Does your partner consistently avoid taking responsibility for their actions?*

14. *Are you frequently subjected to criticism or belittling comments from your partner?*

15. *Does your partner exhibit excessive possessiveness or attempt to control your actions?*

16. *Do you feel like your boundaries and personal space are disregarded by your partner?*

17. *Is decision-making in your relationship characterized by a lack of equality and mutual respect?*

18. *Is there a lack of acceptance or tolerance for your differences in your relationship?*

19. *Do you frequently experience a lack of affection or emotional intimacy from your partner?*

20. *Are you consistently unhappy, fearful, or anxious in your relationship?*

How Do I Solve Unhealthy Relationship Patterns?

Unfortunately, if you answered 'Yes' to some of the above questions, hiding your head in the sand and trying to push onward without addressing what the cause of the issue is and how you can address it will mean a standstill in your relationship harmony. An attempt at ignorance, even if blissful, can lead to a disconnect with yourself and with your partner. The solution to many imbalances and unhealthy patterns is facing them head-on – not just hoping that they will sort themselves out. The following pointers are great ways to start working on beginning to understand yourself more as an individual, to heal, and to grow with your partner:

Identify Your Attachment Style: As explored in Chapter 4, identifying whether you consider your attachment style as secure, anxious, avoidant, or fearful-avoidant can help you learn what you need from a relationship, and how to work both on yourself and with your partner to end the cycle of unhealthy patterns.

Focus on Introspection and Self-Discovery: In the process of identifying your attachment style, consider why you form emotional connections in that way. Consider self-reflection, journaling, self-sabotaging behaviors, and how you set up and maintain your boundaries.

Consider Your Early Family Behavioral Models: Reflect on your childhood and the relationships you were exposed to growing up, as this can help you determine what behaviors you might be unconsciously repeating.

Consider Your Behaviors: It can be easy to shift the blame to your partner for a repeat pattern. Even if you covered the list of questions above and answered 'Yes' to a few, healing relationship patterns also require a hard look at yourself and your behaviors. Are you overly in need of constant communication, and left feeling anxious without it? Are you the one escalating minor situations and turning mountains out of molehills? Consider the part you play in your interactions with your partner, to assess the work on both sides that needs to be done.

Work on Self-Love and Acceptance: It might sound cliché, but working on healing your underlying trauma and building up your self-esteem will leave you feeling more worthy and deserving of love. This requires time and diligent work, so be kind to yourself during the process.

Try Therapy: Doing it alone can be difficult, so where possible, try and involve a therapist. A mental health professional can aid you in identifying negative patterns, help you with self-reflection and the root of your behaviors, and assist you with learning new strategies to help you work through unhealthy relationship patterns.

Abusive Relationships

While you can work on yourself and work with your partner to identify certain behaviors that are causing unhealthy relationship patterns, there is a point where letting go is necessary. While you can work hard at healing your wounds, you are not responsible for healing others, and you cannot save or change people – particularly if they mean and cause you frequent harm. Leaving abusive relationships can be incredibly challenging and sensitive, and if you do consider yourself to be experiencing relationship patterns that are beyond the norm, and are in any danger, consider the following:

Prioritize Your Safety: Your safety should be the top priority. Create a safety plan to protect yourself during and after leaving the relationship. This may involve finding a safe place to stay, informing trusted friends or family members about your situation, and keeping important documents and emergency contact information readily available.

Seek Support: Reach out to trusted friends, family members, or helpline organizations that specialize in supporting survivors of abuse. They can provide emotional support, guidance, and resources to help you through the process.

Choose the Right Time to Leave: Select a time to leave when you believe you will be safest and your departure the most feasible. This might be when the abuser is not present, or with the aid of a friend, family member, or an organization. Avoid interacting with the abuser, and take only vital belongings.

Consider Restraining Orders: Consult with a lawyer or organization to obtain a restraining order or protective order against the abuser.

Cut Contact: Limit or cut off all contact with the abuser. Change your phone number, block their email and social media accounts, and inform people in your life to not share any information about you with them.

Seek Professional Help: Abusive relationships can have immense impacts on mental well-being. Reach out to therapists, counselors, or support groups that specialize in abusive trauma to help you to heal.

Activities

If you and your partner are experiencing repetitive relationship difficulties, the activities below will help you work on opening up to one another and analyzing the causes of these issues.

Relationship Reflections

What are some patterns of behaviors in our relationship that you have found distressing or dissatisfying?

_____

_____

_____

_____

_____

_____

_____

How have these patterns impacted your emotional well-being and our overall relationship?

_____

_____

_____

_____

_____

_____

Can you think of any of your behaviors that might be contributing to these dynamics?

_____

_____

_____

_____

_____

_____

_____

Boundaries and Consent

What are your boundaries, and do you feel like you express them adequately to your partner?

_____

_____

_____

_____

Do you each respect the other's boundaries? Are there any occasions where you feel like these boundaries have been disrespected?

_____

_____

_____

_____

Going forward, are there any ways you could work to acknowledge each other's boundaries and establish a greater degree of understanding and respect?

_____

_____

_____

_____

Introspection

What was your family dynamic like in your childhood? How did your parents/primary caregivers interact?

_____

_____

_____

_____

How do you think these dynamics shaped your understanding of what a healthy relationship looks like?

_____

_____

_____

_____

Do you find yourself repeating or replicating in your relationship?

_____

_____

_____

_____

Self-Care and Personal Growth

What self-care activities do you enjoy, that increase your sense of joy and well-being?

_____

_____

_____

_____

Could you incorporate these activities more, or think of other ways to practice self-care?

_____

_____

_____

_____

Do you have any goals or aspirations that you are working toward? What could you implement to help you work toward these goals?

_____

_____

_____

_____

_____

Have you expressed your goals and self-care practices to your partner?

_____

_____

_____

_____

_____

_____

_____

How can you work toward supporting one another in your individual personal growth?

_____

_____

_____

_____

_____

A great tool to use to improve relationships is to understand your love language and the love language of your partner. You will discover everything about love languages and how to use them to your benefit in the next chapter.

Chapter 6:

Finding and Using Your Love Language

"People tend to criticize their spouse most loudly in the area where they themselves have the deepest emotional need."

— Gary Chapman

What Is a Love Language?

People experience love differently. This extends to how they express love, and how they want to feel loved by others. Individuals might naturally express love languages differently to their partners, so it is important to understand how you best feel loved, and how you can best show your partner that you love them, so you can best show your love to one another.

The Different Love Languages

The term 'love language' has grown in popularity, coined by author Gary Chapman. They are generally divided into the five following categories:

Words of Affirmation: This involves verbalizing affection and appreciation, or incorporating written emotions like love letters. It extends to compliments, praise, and showing how much you value and love a person.

Acts of Service: People whose love language are acts of service value actions over words. They feel loved when their partners assist them with tasks and show effort in action, such as small things like bringing them a cup of coffee, picking them up from the airport, or helping them move to a new house.

Gift Giving: Some individuals value receiving thoughtful gifts as their primary form of love.

Quality Time: Spending meaningful time with loved ones, without distractions, and giving them all your attention is another love language. This can include one-on-one dates, experiences, quality conversations, or any other time when your partner's attention is focused on you.

Physical Touch: This involves expressing love through physical touch, such as hugging, holding hands, kissing, and cuddling.

What Is My Love Language?

Determining your language requires reflecting on what brings you the most reassurance and joy from your partner. It usually is not confined to one love language alone but can be a combination of multiple categories. To assess your love language, reflect on your preferences and answers to the following questions:

Do you enjoy being complimented by your partner?

Do you feel most valued when your partner spends quality time with you?

Do you feel the most appreciated when your partner gives you gifts?

Do you enjoy constant physical touch and affection?

Do you feel the most supported in your relationship when your partner goes out of their way to assist you with tasks?

What Is My Partner's Love Language?

Even if you are aware of how you like to receive love and your love language, being aware of your partner's love language is just as important. To assess your partner's love language, try and answer the following. Most importantly, consider discussing these questions with them to get an open and honest response:

How does your partner respond to words of affirmation such as being reminded that you love them and that you think they are a wonderful person?

_____

_____

_____

_____

How does your partner respond to you performing acts of service such as cleaning their car or tidying on their behalf?

_____

_____

_____

_____

How does your partner respond to gifts you give them?

_____

_____

_____

_____

How does your partner respond to the quality time you both spend together?

_____

_____

_____

_____

_____

Do you notice any patterns in how your partner responds to any of the above? Do any of the ways in which you express love have a more significant emotional impact on them?

_____

_____

_____

_____

How does your partner show affection and love to others?

_____

_____

_____

_____

Does your partner express certain requests for how they wish you to show your affection?

_____

_____

_____

_____

_____

Have you had an open conversation with your partner about what they need to feel the most loved and appreciated?

_____

_____

_____

_____

_____

How Love Languages Can Help Strengthen Relationships

You might find that your love languages are mismatched with your partner's. This is by no means the end of the world or your relationship. Learning and attuning yourself to someone else's love language takes time, and develops as a relationship progresses. Recent studies have also shown that couples with differing love languages have just as healthy relationships as those who share the same language. However, learning your love language and identifying your partner's love language can help strengthen your relationship by allowing you to meet each other's needs. It is crucial for effective communication, enhancing your emotional connection, reducing areas of potential conflict, and allowing you both to thrive in an environment where you feel loved and supported by one another.

How Can I Honor My Partner's Love Language?

If you have managed to conclude how your partner enjoys receiving love, consider some of the following examples of how you can express your love:

Words of Affirmation

- Give them regular compliments like "I appreciate you so much," or "I am so lucky to be with you," or "You look amazing."
- Leave them a note saying "I love you."
- Tell them how proud you are about something they accomplished like "I am so proud of you for ..."

Acts of Service

- Do their laundry for them.
- Bring them breakfast in bed.
- Build their IKEA furniture for them.

Gift Giving

- Send your partner flowers.
- Make them a handmade gift.
- Buy them something they have had their eye on for a while.

Quality Time

- Schedule a regular date night.
- Take a trip together.
- Go on a long walk, to the movies, or try an exercise class together.

Physical Touch

- Regular kisses and cuddles
- Holding hands
- Intimacy

Unhealthy Use of Love Languages

With all your newfound knowledge of your partner's love language, it is also important to be aware of how not to use each other's love languages inappropriately. Sharing your love language with someone is an intimate and emotional experience, and is not to be used in a way to control your partner. Maintaining boundaries and respect within your relationship is always key, particularly when acknowledging one another's love languages and expressing them. The following examples show how love languages might be used in an inappropriate and controlling manner, versus a positive and affirmative way:

Words of Affirmation

- Healthy: You look beautiful today.
- Unhealthy: You should wear more makeup; you look great with it on.

Acts of Service

- Healthy: I picked up your favorite coffee today on my way home.

- Unhealthy: I made you breakfast today, so you owe me and need to clean the house.

Quality Time

- Healthy: I adore spending time with you away from all the outside distractions when we can. It makes me feel so connected to you.
- Unhealthy: You do not need to see your friends. We should spend all of our time together.

Gift Giving

- Healthy: I know you have wanted this bag for a while, so I got it to surprise you.
- Unhealthy: I bought you this gift, it was really expensive and you owe me something in return.

Physical Touch

- Healthy: I feel so uplifted and loved when you spontaneously put your arms around my back.
- Unhealthy: If you will not have sex with me now, you do not properly love me.

Activities

Love Language Quiz

Trying to work out your love language? Try out the following quiz to help assess how and what makes you feel loved and appreciated, or try asking your partner the same questions to gain more insight into their love language.

Which of these would be your dream date?

a. A shopping spree hosted by your partner, for whatever your heart desires
b. Going on a road trip and exploring new places together
c. Creating a jar of written love notes for each other
d. Your partner taking care of all your chores for a day, giving you time off to relax
e. A couple's massage or a night spent cuddling together

How would you like to receive love during a challenging time?

a. Receiving a meaningful gift or something you have been wanting for a while
b. Your partner dedicating an entire day to spend quality time to listen to your thoughts and feelings and make sure you are okay
c. Receiving heartfelt texts and letters to reassure you
d. Your partner taking care of all of your chores and going out of their way to make your day-to-day life easier
e. Frequent cuddles and kisses

What would be your ideal way to celebrate a relationship milestone?

a. Exchanging meaningful and sentimental gifts
b. Planning a grand adventure or unique experience together
c. Writing and performing a song or poem dedicated to your partner
d. Having a day where your partner takes care of all responsibilities, allowing you to relax and enjoy
e. Enjoying a romantic getaway with plenty of opportunities for physical affection

How would you like to receive an apology from your partner?

a. Receiving a heartfelt and thoughtful apology gift

b. Spending quality time together, talking and reconnecting

c. Hearing sincere words of apology and understanding

d. Your partner showing their apology through gestures such as cooking dinner for you, cleaning your car, or sorting out all your bills

e. A big hug and tender affection to show that everything is forgiven

Which romantic gesture would make your heart flutter the most?

a. Your partner surprising you with a personalized love letter hidden in an unexpected place

b. Going on a spontaneous picnic or watching a beautiful sunset together

c. Your partner organizing the entirety of a trip away for you two

d. Your partner taking over your household chores for a week to give you a break

e. Dancing together closely and intimately

Now, tally up your answers:

- If you mostly answered 'a' your love language may be gift-giving.
- If you mostly answered 'b' your love language may be quality time.
- If you mostly answered 'c' your love language may be words of affirmation.
- If you mostly answered 'd' your love language may be acts of service.
- If you mostly answered 'e' your love language may be physical touch.

Discovering your love language and the love language of your partner can be a great tool for strengthening your connection and intimacy. In the next chapter, you will discover more tips for strengthening your connection and intimacy with your partner.

Chapter 7:

Reconnecting and Rekindling Intimacy

"Intimacy is about truth. When you realize you can tell someone your truth, when you can show yourself to them, when you stand in front of them and their response is 'you're safe with me', that's intimacy."

— Taylor Jenkins Reid

Emotionally Reconnecting With Your Partner

G etting your partner to say 'Yes' to being exclusive, proposing, or finalizing whatever form of partnership you have does not mean the hard work is over. Most of the time, it has only just begun. Healthy relationships take constant nurturing and work and require both participants to regularly check in with one another and continue to grow both as individuals and as a team. Keeping your emotional connection alive and thriving is key to fostering a healthy and long-lasting relationship.

Sometimes, you might also feel this emotional connection slipping. Perhaps you have spent a large portion of time apart, or feel like you are on different wavelengths. Whatever the reason, prioritizing your relationship and working on your emotional connection can help you to regain mutual love and respect and revive your love for one another.

Ways to Emotionally Reconnect With Your Partner

Working on emotionally reconnecting with your partner requires effort and consideration. The below suggestions will help you find the best approach for your relationship:

Communicate: Perhaps the most important point I have stressed throughout this book is open communication. If you feel your connection slipping or your relationship is ill at ease, let your partner know. Talking openly and being honest with your emotions will allow you both to work together through these issues as a team. Try to find time daily to check in with your partner, if only for a few minutes, as this can help foster a consistent connection and help you both feel fully involved in each other's lives. Additionally, do not avoid bringing up heavy topics. Even if you are worried, you have doubts, or something is upsetting you, being honest with your partner and discussing these feelings is key to overcoming them. Using the active listening and conflict resolution techniques explored earlier, you should be well-equipped to bring up difficult topics and work through them as a team.

Change It Up: Monotony can breed boredom, so changing things up and keeping it interesting is key to a long-lasting relationship. Life can be busy and can get in the way of a relationship, but it is important to refocus your priority on your partner to stay connected. Consider different date nights, new experiences, and otherwise breaking out of routine so you can share new experiences and continue to foster your emotional connection.

Consider How You Can Support Your Partner: If you do feel like your connection has slipped, reflect on what you can do to better support your partner. This can be in a workbook or journal, or a mental list. Use some of the love language techniques explored in the previous chapter and consider how you can tailor expressing your affection to your partner and reminding them of your love.

Be Ready to Show Remorse: Owning up and saying sorry can sometimes be difficult. It is also usually not worth saying if you do not mean it, as it can come across as shallow and ineffective. However, work on accepting your part in any issues that arise and acknowledging how you might have contributed to certain issues. After reflecting on them, try and openly communicate and apologize to your partner in an honest and remorseful way.

Never Threaten to Leave in a Bid to Get Your Partner to Beg You to Stay: Things are difficult, you are having a hard time communicating, and you feel rejected. You might feel tempted to cry wolf and threaten to leave the relationship. However, never use this threat, unless you mean it, as it is highly manipulative and overall a poor approach to trying to get your partner on the same page. Instead, work on openly communicating your issues and cooperating with your partner to find solutions.

Acknowledge When You Are Being Overly Emotional or Reactive: Sometimes, you are the bad guy. You might find yourself blowing up unnecessarily over small things, or going through extended periods of callousness or emotional sensitivity. Be ready to acknowledge when this happens, admit it to your partner, and take a step back to cool off before you return to any issues at hand.

Practice Random Acts of Kindness: If you feel like you are struggling with a lack of emotional connection, consider how you can express your love to your partner through spontaneous acts of kindness. Incorporate their love language in the process; text them to tell them you love them, send them flowers, and kiss them before you leave for work. Practicing active appreciation daily can help immensely restore and rekindle the emotional connection.

When Should You Ask for Help?

If you do find yourself struggling in your relationship, repeating the same unhealthy patterns, constantly in conflict, or otherwise unable to resolve issues, consider involving a therapist or counselor. Early intervention is often the best approach in these situations, and even couples who consider their relationship stable and healthy may benefit from the assistance of a couples therapist. Reaching out and asking for help is never a failure, but instead, an effective way to combat any issues and restore your emotional connection.

Rekindling Intimacy

Having a great deal of sex early on in your relationship is pretty common. Having less sex after you begin to merge your lives, live together, and grow increasingly busy, perhaps after also the introduction of a baby, is equally common. Your private life is suddenly interrupted, priorities change, and it is harder to find and spend quality time together. Discussing your sex life is key, even if you might find it a little bit awkward. Being open and honest with your partner about your desires and your boundaries will help you stay on the same page about how you are feeling, what is working, and what is amiss. Consider the following questions:

Is there anything you would like to try or experiment with?

_____

_____

_____

_____

_____

Is there anything you would like to do more or less?

_____

_____

_____

_____

_____

What sexual experiences or activities have you enjoyed with your partner?

_____

_____

_____

_____

_____

How emotionally connected are you currently feeling with your partner?

_____

_____

_____

_____

_____

What Causes a Lack of Intimacy?

For a variety of reasons, intimacy can also suffer in relationships. Infidelity is a big one, and if you choose to continue your relationship, the process of rebuilding trust and intimacy is extensive. Stress can also get in the way. Being overburdened at work or feeling like you are being pulled in many directions can leave you struggling to relax and engage physically with your partner. Pornography additionally can hurt sex drives. Self-esteem or mental health issues can also cause a person to withdraw and feel disengaged from physical intimacy.

Relationships often go through periods where intimacy is less frequent, and immediately panicking if this happens is often not beneficial. However, if it grows into a regular and consistent issue, it is important to be aware and address it with your partner.

How to Rekindle Intimacy

If you are struggling with intimate connections within your relationship, consider the following:

Consider the Cause: If the cause of the lack of physical intimacy is at first unclear, try and reflect on what might be causing it.

Are you or your partner overly busy and stressed?

_____

_____

Do you or your partner experience self-esteem issues or mental health issues?

_____

_____

Are there any other changes in your relationship that might have led to a reduced level of physical intimacy?

_____

_____

_____

_____

Communicate: Talk openly with your partner about how you are feeling, your desires, and your boundaries. Set a space where you can both share your feelings and reflect on each other's perspectives. Identify also what you need to feel aroused. For women, this is often a more extensive process. It can range from a slow and gradual date night, to light touching and emotional intimacy, building slowly up to feeling aroused.

Prioritize Spending Time With One Another: Try and set regular time aside for your partner to spend quality time. This does not have to be centered on intimacy; it could be a date, a dinner, or any other form of time spent together without distractions. This can be hard in marriage, particularly with children, but work where possible to set time aside to focus on one another.

Shake Things Up: Long-term couples might find themselves in a monotonous pattern of having brief sex at the same time, which can lead to a great deal of boredom and dissatisfaction. Consider changing your routine, trying new things, and being open to exploration.

Consider Who Is Initiating: Relationships often involve one individual who is more likely to initiate sex. If this applies to you, consider reversing roles and having the individual who infrequently initiates sexual intimacy try pursuing it.

Practice Self-Care: Feeling sexy can go a long way, so working to take care of your mental and physical health is key to raising your self-esteem and increasing your libido.

Broaden Your Definition of Intimacy: The definition of intimacy is often limited to intercourse, penetration, and orgasms. This does not have to be the case. Work on foreplay and other forms of physical intimacy; kissing, massaging, and cuddling. All forms of physicality can work to foster and rekindle intimacy and strengthen your emotional bond.

Consider Counseling: Reaching out to a counselor or therapist can be incredibly useful in navigating issues such as a change in physical intimacy, and professionals can often provide tailored, expert advice on how to resolve your issues.

How to Rekindle Intimacy After Infidelity

If you do find yourself betrayed in a relationship, or even engaged in infidelity yourself, and you both choose to stay and work through these issues, physical intimacy is often a hard step to overcome. Consider the following when working toward rekindling intimacy after trust has been lost:

Make Sure the Betrayal Is Over: Whether you have been betrayed or have engaged in infidelity yourself, making sure that the indiscretion is over before attempting to rekindle physical intimacy is key. This means, naturally, making sure the affair or cheating is over, cutting all contact, and doing whatever is necessary to cut all ties with the transgression.

Take Time to Heal: If you are on the receiving end of infidelity, be kind to yourself. Being betrayed by a spouse or partner is often heartbreaking, and taking the time to grieve and work toward healing yourself is key to moving on and repairing your relationship.

Communicate: Some things can be difficult to hear. Before asking for intimate details about an affair or cheating, consider if you want to know all the details. However, communicating about why it took place is crucial. Are there issues in your relationship that require addressing? Are you or your partner facing struggles or temptations that require professional help? This will likely be an intensely emotional and upsetting conversation, which can create a huge amount of conflict, but is key to rebuilding broken trust.

Construct Boundaries: Once you have addressed the transgression and its causes, and taken the time to emotionally process the situation, it is time to start rebuilding your relationship. This means reinforcing boundaries and communicating honestly. This might also mean new boundaries being set in place; perhaps sharing passwords, sharing locations, and sharing bank statements. All of these boundaries will be individual to your situation and require the active participation of both individuals to construct.

Rekindle Your Love: Even if you have been deeply wounded, if you are choosing to stay in your relationship, try and remind yourself why you chose your partner and all the characteristics that you appreciate in them. Prioritize spending quality time together to create new memories and rekindle a wounded passion.

Gradually Reintroduce Physical Intimacy: If you have been cheated on or betrayed, you might well not want to engage in sex for a good while. However, the pace at which sexual intimacy is reintroduced into the relationship is dependent on the wounded party. They should be allowed to lead, set boundaries, and move at the pace they are comfortable with.

Activities

Questions for Building Emotional Intimacy:

If you are experiencing issues with intimately connecting with your partner, consider the following questions:

What is one thing you appreciate most about our relationship and why?

_____

_____

_____

_____

_____

_____

If we were to describe our love story using emojis, which ones would you choose?

_____

What is a goal or dream you have that you have not shared with me yet?

_____

_____

_____

If we could have a themed date night, what theme would you choose and why?

_____

_____

_____

What is the most memorable adventure or spontaneous moment we have had together?

_____

_____

_____

_____

If we were to create a bucket list of experiences to share, what would be your top 3 items?

_____

_____

_____

What is the most valuable lesson you have learned from a past relationship?

_____

_____

_____

Where do you see us in 5 years?

_____

_____

_____

_____

What is something about yourself that you want me to understand better?

_____

_____

_____

What goals do you have for our relationship?

_____

_____

_____

_____

What is the most hilarious or embarrassing thing that has ever happened to us as a couple?

_____

_____

_____

_____

If we could travel back in time to any era, which one would you choose and why?

_____

_____

_____

What is one thing that you find irresistibly cute or attractive about me?

_____

_____

_____

What was your first impression of me?

_____

_____

_____

_____

What is the most meaningful or memorable gift you have ever received from someone?

_____

_____

What were your first words as a child?

_____

_____

What is one thing you have always wanted to ask me but have not yet?

_____

_____

What did you dream about being when you were younger?

_____

_____

_____

How do you think we/our relationship has changed in the past year?

_____

_____

_____

_____

If we were to have a game night, which game would you want to play and why?

_____

_____

_____

What is the most profound or life-changing experience you have had that shaped who you are today?

_____

_____

_____

If we were to have a spontaneous road trip, which destination would you want us to explore?

_____

_____

_____

What is one thing you have learned about yourself since being in a relationship with me?

_____

_____

_____

_____

If we were to write a love letter to each other, what would be the opening line?

_____

_____

_____

What is the funniest or most embarrassing moment from your school days that still makes you laugh?

_____

_____

_____

_____

If we could invent a quirky tradition unique to our relationship, what would it be?

_____

_____

_____

What is a book or movie that has had a significant impact on your outlook on life and why?

_____

_____

_____

_____

If you could have a pet that is not a traditional pet, what animal would you choose?

_____

_____

What trait do you admire in me that you wish you could cultivate more in yourself?

_____

_____

What is one thing you appreciate about the way we handle disagreements and how can we continue to improve our conflict resolution skills?

_____

_____

_____

_____

_____

_____

There is a lot more to a relationship than intimacy, and it is common for conflict to arise in any relationship. In the next chapter, I will be covering the most common issues that can occur in a relationship and what you can do to resolve them.

Chapter 8:

6 Common Conflicts in Relationships and How to Work Through Them

"It seems a lot of relationships fail, because when tough times come around ... People want to give up too easy. The fact of the matter is every relationship is going to experience difficult times sooner or later. Don't throw away a potential good lasting relationship just because things got a little hard."

— Bryan Burden

All relationships go through periods of struggle, but they do not have to be deal breakers. Of course, this not always applies. Consider your boundaries and what you do consider deal breakers, for example, abuse, not wanting children, extreme distrust, and repeated infidelity.

Hopefully, you have been provided with plenty of knowledge on certain relationship patterns, how to resolve conflict, how to express and receive love, and other vital elements of what it takes to make a healthy relationship. However, there are many other instances where you could experience conflict or strife beyond the above, where you will have to put your conflict-resolving skills to the test. In the sections that follow, I will share some common additional instigators of relationship conflict and ways you and your partner can work toward solving them.

If you are experiencing conflict or other problems in your relationship, remember not to panic. Relationships are largely a marathon, not a race, and putting time and effort into solving short-term issues will be greatly beneficial in helping you build a mutually respectful and loving partnership.

Conflict #1: Working Through Difficult Money Matters

We have all heard the saying, "Money is the root of all evil." Particularly in the current economy, financial worries can dominate many aspects of life. This can lead to a great deal of stress and constant worry, both for individuals and for couples who share financial burdens. Financial stress extends to numerous causes, including debt, mortgages, unexpected expenses like sudden hospital bills, financing schools, and many others.

The emotional impact of financial stress can be immense. Constantly living from paycheck to paycheck, worrying about rent increases, and having money on your mind can leave you feeling drained, tired, frustrated, and otherwise ill at ease in your life. Mental health often also suffers as a result of financial stress. Those undergoing worries concerning finances can suffer a great deal of shame, perhaps for not being able to provide, or fear for not being able to continue their quality of life. Additional outcomes from financial stress may include:

- Depression can commonly result from financial stress, as people are left feeling hopeless and weighed down.
- Individuals might also experience unhealthy coping habits such as turning to substance abuse, drinking, gambling, or self-harm.
- Mood swings or excessive outbursts of anger can result from the burden of money worries.
- Insomnia is common in those experiencing financial stress, as worrying thoughts keep them awake at night.
- Anxiety can arise in individuals suffering from financial stress, with symptoms ranging from shaking, sweating, and restlessness, to even panic attacks
- Physical side effects can arise from financial stress. The body often mirrors the mind, and individuals might find themselves experiencing digestive issues, headaches, high blood pressure, or diabetes. The worry of financing healthcare may also prevent

these individuals suffering from attending hospital appointments.

- Suicidal thoughts can arise in individuals deeply burdened by financial worries.

How Financial Stress Can Impact Relationships

Financial stress can also have a detrimental impact on relationships, particularly when couples share finances, experience financial imbalances, or otherwise have to coordinate their earning and spending habits.

Deciding Whose Money Is Whose: Is your money your own? Do you share everything? Do you have separate bank accounts? Is there a pre-nuptial agreement in play? Deciding how to organize and split finances can be difficult, and can cause conflict between individuals. Communicating your ideals and establishing an agreement on your financial views is crucial, particularly before marriage.

Debt: No surprise, but debt can be a huge impediment to relationships. Educational debt or credit card spending can lead to one partner carrying more debt than the other, or a situation where both individuals burden a worrisome amount of debt.

Spending Habits: An austere and frugal partner will have quite the time engaging with someone who loves to treat themselves and to spend. Spending habits vary and can cause conflict and disagreements between partners.

Power Struggle: One partner works, the other does not, one partner is temporarily unemployed, or one partner makes considerably more than the other. All of these factors can lead to conflict and issues in the power dynamic within a relationship.

Children: Providing for children adds a whole extra category of financial worry. Parents might also hold different views on spending when it comes to their children; private school, cars, and extracurricular activities.

Ways to Cope With Financial Stress in a Relationship

Money and finances are sensitive issues but should be openly spoken about and considered by individuals engaging in long-term relationships. Debt and financial stressors are heavy burdens to bear, but a burden shared is often a burden halved.

Develop a Strategy for Dealing With Your Debt and Budgeting: If you do have considerable debt, approach it head-on. Work with your partner to formulate a saving plan. This also involves being wholly open and honest with your partner about your debt and spending habits and devising comprehensive budgets for your lifestyle.

Consider Signing a Prenup/Postnup: A prenuptial agreement is a contract whereby couples agree on how assets and debts should be divided should a marriage end. This can be a tough topic to bring up with a partner, particularly if you are head over heels in love and do not want to even contemplate the idea of things ending, but is a worthwhile consideration for financial protection. Additionally, postnuptial agreements cover the same grounds, signed after marriage or entering into a partnership.

Set Boundaries: If you do share finances, set firm and clear boundaries around spending. This does not have to mean monitoring your partner's bank statement down to every morning coffee, but being aware of each other's spending habits and what is and is not deemed acceptable in terms of spending from a joint bank account.

Be Conscious of Power Play: In a relationship of financial inequality, where for example one partner has considerably more money than the other, be conscious of power struggles. Feeling less well-off or reliant on your partner can breed feelings of resentment, as can having to live your life by the rules of a partner who earns far more and thus makes all of the big decisions in your joint life. Be conscious of your interactions when it comes to spending and net worth, and try and find a way whereby you can both feel equal when it comes to your relationship positioning, even in the case of disproportionate income or value.

Consider Your Financial Approach: Financial views are a form of compatibility. Be open with your partner on how you feel about spending, how you were raised, and what your idea for the future looks like. Want a big house? An annual trip to the Maldives? Or do you want to scrimp and save and build up a nest egg to provide for your children or your rainy days? All of these are important considerations, and being honest with your partner will help you find common ground in navigating finances while in a relationship.

Budgeting and Finances Activity

Stressing about money? Sitting down and assessing your inflows and outflows is important. If you have not already done so, have a go at the following questions to assess your spending habits and what you might be able to save or splash on, while keeping your financial goals in mind.

What are your current sources of income?

For you:

For your partner:

What are your current monthly expenses?

_____

What are your short-term financial goals?

_____

_____

_____

_____

What are your long-term financial goals?

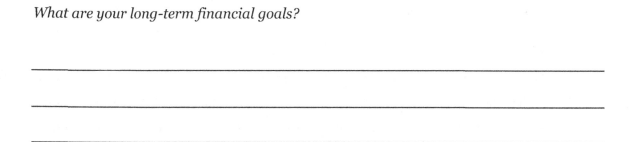

Try and create a monthly budget (if you do not already do so), taking into account your current income, expenses, and what you are saving up for together. Consider using additional resources such as apps, spreadsheets, or old-fashioned pen and paper, and try and stay consistent with your spending habits, with frequent reviews to keep track of how your finances are looking.

Conflict #2: Working Past Infidelity

Infidelity can mean many things, particularly in a society where emotional affairs come at the ease of a click of a button; texting, snapchatting, and emails. Individuals define infidelity differently and will have boundaries when it comes to what they consider cheating and what not. However, when that boundary is crossed, and infidelity does occur, it can often be a dealbreaker in relationships. Working through infidelity and repairing trust after an affair, whether physical or emotional, is immensely difficult. Many couples choose also to part ways after infidelity has taken place, as trust is so difficult to rebuild. However, if you decide to work through a break in trust or transgression, the below pointers will be helpful.

Why Do People Cheat?

It is not to be excused, and it is often one of the most heartbreaking acts you can commit toward your partner, as infidelity tends to eradicate any trust built up within a relationship.

However, some of the potential causes of cheating and infidelity are wise to know, and look out for.

Falling Out of Love: Long-term relationships can lead to ups and downs in the degree to which couples experience mutual affection. Honeymoon phases often involve immense passion, which gradually turns into a stronger, longer lasting, but more leveled-out degree of emotional intimacy. For some couples, this can propel them to feel bored or less attached to their partner, leading them to engage in affairs or cheating.

Commitment Issues: Individuals who struggle with commitment may be more likely to engage in infidelity, even if they value and love their partner.

Low Self-Esteem: Those who struggle with low self-esteem might find themselves seeking the booster of praise and feeling wanted by someone other than their partner. Having sex with a new person can lead to feeling wanted, desired, and attractive.

Mental Health Issues: Mental health issues such as depression or anxiety can also contribute to individuals engaging in cheating as means of self-soothing or other negative solutions to their internal issues.

Major Life Changes: Sudden life changes such as having a baby, not seeing your partner for an extended period, or the loss of a loved one can leave one or both partners feeling emotionally disconnected, which in turn can lead to infidelity.

Sexual Desire and Lack of Impulse Control: People have different sex drives. Those who do have a higher sex drive may be driven to cheat, particularly if they lack the impulse control needed for a committed relationship.

Unmet Needs: Couples might find their sex drives differ. Emotional needs might also differ, leading to individuals seeking out emotional support and connection through online affairs or other forms of infidelity.

Seeking Variety: Individuals in long-term relationships might find themselves craving different conversations, different interactions, and just something new to what they experience with their current partner. In some cases, non-monogamy is also a healthy way to continue a relationship – although this requires both parties to agree to open their relationship – and never an excuse for cheating unless agreed on prior.

What to Do if You Have Cheated on Your Partner

If you are the party who has been involved in some form of transgression, consider whether you still want to continue your current relationship, and your motives behind having cheated.

- Additionally, even if you decide you want to continue your relationship, be aware that your partner may very well not want to.
- The road to rebuilding trust after infidelity is long and hard, and you will have to be prepared to put a great deal of work into supporting your partner and meeting their requirements for rebuilding trust.
- If you do think you are unlikely to be able to avoid cheating in the future, be open with your partner. Infidelity and cheating are greatly damaging to the suffering partner's self-esteem, and putting someone you love through that repeatedly is not a healthy or respectful way to engage in love.
- Consider therapy. Repeatedly cheating and lacking impulse control can often only be managed with the help of a professional.

What to Do if You Have Been Cheated On

Being on the receiving end of infidelity is often heartbreaking. Building up your dreams with your partner, only to have them crumble after that person breaks your trust, is immensely difficult to process. Being cheated on can also damage an individual's self-esteem, can change their views on the world, on trust, and have a multitude of negative consequences such as mental health problems. If you do experience this happening to you, remind yourself of the following:

Do Not Blame Yourself: If you find out you have been cheated on, do not blame yourself. Internalizing infidelity as a 'you' problem can cause deep self-esteem issues. Often, the cause lies instead in other areas, or with your partner, so try to avoid feeling like you caused them to stray and are in some way lacking yourself.

Ask Yourself if You Still Want to Be in the Relationship: Can you forgive your partner? You might very well want to end the relationship after infidelity occurs, which is perfectly natural. However, think deeply about whether you do want to continue your relationship with them, and if you can work to forgive them. Continuing a relationship in which you remain in a constant state of fear regarding your partner cheating will not be beneficial to anyone, so ask yourself if you do want to stay and rebuild that trust.

Ask Your Partner if They Still Want to Continue the Relationship: You might want to stay, but if your partner cheated, they may well not. Communicate openly about why the infidelity occurred, and if your partner also sees a future with you.

Prioritize Yourself: Put yourself first for a while. Do not be afraid to set firmer boundaries and express your needs. Need time out from the relationship? Ask for it. Need to have their social passwords? Get them. Need your partner to come to couples therapy? Do so. This is a time to put yourself first and work with the support of your partner to heal.

Do Not Stay out of the Fear of Being Alone: If you want to leave, do so. Staying in a relationship where one partner is continuing to cheat is immensely unhealthy, and staying in that relationship out of fear will only construct a partnership of toxicity and distrust.

Create a Support Network and Talk to a Therapist: Working past infidelity requires a strong network of friends and other trusted individuals. You might be worried about sharing the infidelity with them but be open and allow others to support you. This may also extend to mental health professionals who can help you work through your feelings and try to help heal both you and your relationship.

Consider asking your partner the following questions to openly communicate about where you stand after such a transgression:

How do you feel about me?

_____

_____

_____

_____

How do you feel about the person you had an affair with/cheated with?

_____

_____

_____

_____

_____

Is our relationship worth fighting for?

_____

_____

_____

_____

Has anything changed in our relationship that caused this?

_____

_____

_____

_____

What is it about me and our relationship that makes this worth repairing?

_____

_____

_____

_____

_____

_____

Forgiving Infidelity

If you do decide to forgive your partner and move forwards, be prepared for the long road ahead. Rebuilding trust will take effort and commitment from both sides. Consider posing the partner who cheated the following questions to open up to one another about the infidelity:

Do you regret the infidelity?

_____

_____

Would you still be continuing to cheat if it had not been discovered?

_____

_____

How do you feel about how it has impacted me?

_____

_____

_____

_____

_____

_____

Why did you start cheating?

_____

_____

_____

_____

How did you justify that within our relationship, to yourself?

_____

_____

_____

_____

You are likely experiencing a host of emotions, but if you do consider forgiving your partner for infidelity, work on the following:

Communicate With Your Partner: As calmly as possible once you have processed your feelings, discuss the questions above and work on trying to establish the reasons behind the affair and how you can move forwards.

Set Boundaries: As mentioned above, have the confidence to ask for what you need moving forwards. Assess what will make you feel most comfortable and express these to your partner.

Involve a Couples Therapist: Outside mediation and professional can go a long way in helping couples heal and move past infidelity.

What Forgiveness Is Not

While you might be open to working with your partner to repair your relationship and might be ready to forgive, this does not mean that once you have told your partner you have forgiven them, the work is over. Forgiveness is just the first step in rebuilding trust after a betrayal.

You Are Not Saying That You Will Never Be Upset Again: Emotions will likely continue to rise after an affair or cheating has taken place. Your partner should be open and aware of this, and ready to support you when you do need to bring up your hurt and feelings again. Forgiveness does not eradicate the act that has taken place and does not mean that the betrayed partner is over the trauma that they have experienced.

You Are Not Excusing Their Actions: Forgiveness is also not saying that cheating is acceptable. Separating a willingness to heal and move forwards, while maintaining how much your partner hurt you, is difficult. However, maintaining a distinction between the two will help you organize your feelings and uphold your values.

You Are Not Ready to Completely Trust Them: You might forgive, but you do not forget. Practicing forgiveness and expressing this to your partner is different from being able to commit to fully trusting that person again. This may well not be possible. However, while forgiveness is a big step toward rebuilding a relationship, it is not the same as sweeping the issue under the rug and forgetting about it.

Rebuilding Trust After Infidelity

Forgiveness might have taken place, but trust is often harder to rebuild. In working toward rebuilding trust with your partner, consider the following:

Open Communication: Be ready to check in regularly to make sure the cheating is not still taking place, but ultimately, you will also want to get to a place where you do not have to ask nor monitor their every move. Nonetheless, try to communicate as openly as possible.

Self-Care: Look after yourself. You are likely wounded, so practicing self-care and doing things that make you happy will help you feel good, to bring renewed energy to rebuilding trust with your partner.

Keep Promises You Made to Yourself: Did you say you would leave if they cheated again? Then do so. Avoid setting internal boundaries and then bending them if transgressions occur. Some people cannot change, no matter how much you love them.

Be Patient: Rebuilding trust takes time. It will not happen overnight, and there may be setbacks along the way, but be ready for a long journey to rebuilding that trust.

Conflict #3: Working Through Parenting Conflicts

If your relationship involves dependents, you might well find parenting conflicts a common and difficult issue. Holding the responsibility for a child is difficult enough. Sharing this responsibility might initially be considered at times easier, but can lead to issues when disagreements arise over parenting approaches. This can affect children of all forms of relationship, including non-married parental figures, divorced or separated parents, adoptive parents, sex-sex parents, or foster parents.

Below is a selection of common issues and scenarios in which parents experience conflict when approaching their role and working alongside their partner:

Different Rules and Expectations: Everyone tends to have a different approach to parenting, often based on how they were raised themselves and how they view the ideal way to raise children of their own. This might be shaped by an attempt to replicate their childhood; they had a stay-at-home parent figure, thus want the same for their children.

Alternatively, parents might strongly wish to eradicate elements of their childhood when parenting their children. As children of parents who were not overly involved in their lives, they might grow to become overbearing in the lives of their children.

Parents might also come into conflict over basic rules. One parent figure demands the child finish their vegetables, the other believes this to be detrimental to their outlook on eating. One parent demands that their child excel at school and should go on to have a successful and respected career, the other believes they should pursue their dreams.

Favoritism: Although they might be unwilling to admit it, parents can be susceptible to feeling and showing favoritism toward one child over the other (if multiple children are involved). Additionally, parents can find themselves competing for the affection of their children, even if only on a subconscious level.

Disciplinary Issues: Parents might also differ in their views on how to discipline their children, and differentiation in each parent's approach can lead to conflict. In response to catching a child lying, or stealing a bag of sweets, one parent suggests removing their PlayStation or phone for a week. The other raises their voice, yells and shouts, and seizes all electronic devices for a month. Differing views on how to respond to discipline can also cause issues as parents then find themselves unable to approach misbehavior as a united front, causing issues for both parents and child.

Financial Concerns: For all the reasons mentioned above, the sudden inclusion of an additional family member can cause a great deal more stress and pressure on a couple, leading to increased conflict and worry about how to provide.

Additionally, remain aware that problems unrelated to children can lead to increased parental conflict. Issues within relationships, marriages, and partnerships, can also filter out into family life and cause unnecessary strife.

Impact of Parental Conflict on Children

Parental conflict can have a detrimental impact on the health and well-being of children, and it is worth considering the extent of these impacts when assessing your relationship with your partner and how you navigate parenthood.

Mental and Emotional Impact: Recurring conflict between parents can lead to a great deal of stress for children, in turn leading to mental health issues such as depression and anxiety, as well as many additional issues such as acting out, concentrating less at school, poor self-esteem, or disinterest in socializing.

Children Feel Pushed to Take Sides: In the case of being present between two arguing parental figures, children may be pushed to feel like they have to side with one over the other. This can cause a huge rift in family life, and leave children feeling increasingly ashamed and guilty.

Decreased Quality of Parenting and Family Unity: Ongoing parental conflict can decrease the effectiveness of parenting skills, as parents lose sight of the real focus –the well-being of their children – and find themselves at times too otherwise absorbed in the ongoing conflict. This can leave children feeling neglected and unseen, and decrease the ability of all family members to bond and grow together.

Poor Role-Modeling: Children base a lot of their characterizations and behaviors on how they see their parents behaving. Parents who are constantly in disagreement over parenting approaches and other issues can lead them to grow up in an environment where they feel confused and unsafe. This can also have long-lasting impacts on how children construct their relationships as adults, as previously mentioned. Children growing up in a household of hostility and conflict may well be inclined to try and construct a similar environment in adulthood and be drawn to partners with whom they clash themselves.

How to Reduce Parental Conflict in a Relationship

When working to reduce any disagreement in parenting approaches with your partner, consider the following:

Define a Collaborative Parenting Approach and Create Rules Together: Be open and honest with your partner on your ideals and values, and how you want to approach parenting. This might require extensive discussions into even minor details such as screen time, homework importance, bedtimes, and many others. Formulating a parenting plan together will mean that you can work as a team and united front in raising your children, and avoid any potential conflict in areas where you might see differently. On the areas where you do find yourselves disagreeing, try to come to a mutual agreement and compromise. Parenting duties also involve a great deal of flexibility; knowing when to give and when to take. Know and maintain your boundaries when it comes to your parenting approach, but also be conscious of your partner's ideals and upbringing, and try and formulate a new and personal plan that incorporates the best of both of you.

Agree on a Disciplinary Approach: Following on from formulating a parenting plan together, get on the same page as to how you will enforce discipline and consequences for your children. Again, this might require extensive communication and explanations behind your reasonings but will be beneficial in the long run and reduce potential conflict over disciplinary approaches.

Work as a Team: Having formulated your parenting plan and your disciplinary approach, be ready to work together and back each other up when needed. Children benefit from seeing their parents work together, seeing them support one another, and being privy to how they are capable of navigating life as a unit. This also reduces any feelings children might experience regarding the need to side with one parent over the other.

Avoid Arguing in Front of Your Children: Conflict and arguments will still happen, but try to have these behind closed doors, away from your children. Additionally, use your coping techniques to avoid engaging in emotional reactiveness or aggression, such as raising your voice or getting otherwise physical. Consider the impression you are setting for your child, and keep your disagreements for when you are alone with your partner.

Avoid Involving Your Children in Arguments: Again, should arguments arise, at no point should you try to recruit your children in the battle against your partner. Doing this will only amplify feelings of guilt and confusion. Keep disagreements to yourselves and work on them in your alone time, using the conflict resolution skills mentioned previously.

Parenting Struggles Activity

If you are struggling with finding a way to parent cohesively with your partner, try out the following questions:

Challenges

Can you identify specific parenting challenges that you are currently experiencing in your relationship?

_____

_____

_____

_____

_____

_____

Values

Does your parenting approach differ from that of your partner? If so, in what ways?

_____

_____

_____

_____

_____

_____

In what ways is your parenting style similar to that of your partner?

_____

_____

_____

_____

_____

_____

Parenting Plan

Work with your partner to try and establish a collaborative parenting plan (if you have not already done so). Consider the following:

How you will approach discipline

_____

_____

_____

How you will approach expectations

_____

_____

_____

How you will divide up tasks and responsibilities

_____

_____

_____

How you can support one another in parenting

_____

_____

Conflict #4: Working Through Past Traumas

Entering into a committed, long-term relationship often means opening up about past traumas, when that person feels comfortable. For some, this can take years. Some may never feel ready to share their past traumas with their partner. However, getting to a point of mutual trust where you can open up and share experiences that have greatly impacted your life can be beneficial to healing. Sharing these with your partner can help them better understand you and your behavior, and how you approach your relationship.

What Is Trauma?

Trauma is generally regarded as a long-lasting emotional response to a frightening or distressing event. How people respond to events and experiences varies, so traumatic events can be difficult to define. Experiencing traumatic events can shape an individual's sense of self-esteem, and their ability to connect to others, form relationships, and regulate their own emotions. Extreme trauma can lead to post-traumatic stress disorder, otherwise known as PTSD.

Examples of trauma (not limited to):

- Emotional or physical abuse
- Sexual abuse
- Being neglected as a child
- Traumatic events such as a car crash
- Sudden loss of a loved one
- Domestic violence or abuse
- Natural disaster
- Racism

How Trauma Impacts Relationships

As traumatic events can have such an impact on how we behave and relate to others, they can also affect our romantic relationships – particularly if left undressed. For example, being sexually abused might affect an individual's ability to engage in physical touch, let alone be intimate. Being neglected can lead to anxious or avoidant attachment styles and a fear of trusting others, or a desperate need for co-dependency and constant reassurance. A person who has been through serious life events, such as war or natural disaster, might suffer from flashbacks or intense anxiety, and struggle to regulate their mood in the presence of their partner. All of these have long-lasting impacts on how individuals navigate future relationships and can be detrimental if left unaddressed.

How Can I Help My Partner With Their Trauma?

It is important to accept that you are not your partner's therapist, nor a professional, and should they need professional support, this should be encouraged. Supporting a person who is struggling and suffers from trauma on your own is often too large a burden to bear.

However, supporting someone who has lacked love in their life, or showing someone who has been hurt, wounded, or had their trust broken that consistent and valuable love does exist does wonders to heal old wounds. Here are some things you can do to support your partner in working through their trauma when they do feel confident in opening up to you:

Be Patient and Listen When They Are Ready: When your partner does feel comfortable opening up (and you should not push them), listen wholeheartedly and without judgment or interruption. Accept and acknowledge any feelings they might share, and reassure them that you still love them.

Educate Yourself on Your Partner's Trauma: Once the trauma has been shared, do your research. Educate yourself on how people who have been exposed to this particular type of trauma respond, and how you can best support your partner. Identify their triggers and work on supporting them throughout your relationship.

Maintain Your Boundaries: Supporting someone who has been through a traumatic past takes immense compassion and patience. However, be aware of your boundaries, and do not let their behavior affect you in a way that is beyond your comfort. Enabling their behavior will often be detrimental to both individuals, as will forming a relationship whereby an individual with a history of trauma is wholly reliant on their partner, so much so that they begin to overwhelm them. Know when to step back and enforce what you need to be able to support them in the best way possible.

Identifying Your Triggers Activity

This can apply to both anything you are holding on to from your relationship, and past traumatic experiences. Identifying your triggers can be immensely helpful in being able to avoid them in the future, or use the self-soothing practices below to calm yourself if you do find your emotions rising.

What situations that you have been in with your partner or behaviors they have exhibited have had a strong emotional impact on you?

_____

_____

_____

_____

_____

How did you feel when those triggers were activated?

_____

_____

_____

_____

_____

Reflect on your past experiences. Is there any link between these and how you respond to your relationship triggers?

_____

_____

_____

_____

_____

Have you discussed these triggers with your partner?

_____

_____

_____

_____

Conflict #5: Having Different Values

People have different values, different morals, and different belief systems. When combining those into a relationship, it can be difficult to navigate differences. Many people are initially drawn to partners who exhibit characteristics completely different from their own but can over time grow to find these disparities frustrating and find themselves in conflict over areas of disagreement, or attempting to change their partner. The important thing is to always remember that everyone is individual and that you should celebrate each other's differences – not try to eradicate these differences.

If you do find yourselves in conflict over differences, remember the following:

Talk About Your Differences: The most important approach to overcoming disagreements is talking about them. Communicate openly and practice the active listening techniques we have covered.

Try and See Your Partner's Perspective: Use your empathy knowledge to try and put yourself in your partner's shoes. Why do they feel the way that they feel? Reflect on what potential elements have caused their belief system, as well as your own.

Meet in the Middle: Finding a balance between maintaining your moral values and boundaries and accommodating your partner is difficult, but be willing to be flexible where possible, share and debate ideas, and try and find a compromise that suits you both. In making these adjustments, be prepared to give and take. If you sacrifice something for your partner to adjust to their lifestyle, expect the same in return and vice versa to foster a system of equality.

Do Not Force It: You cannot instill or force a belief upon your partner. Some things you just will not see eye to eye on, and that you need to accept.

Agree to Disagree: On core values and ideas you cannot come to a compromise on (and should not – core values should never be compromised), agree to disagree, and work toward accepting each other as individuals with differing perspectives. Try to reshape your perspective and see your partner's contrasting beliefs as bringing a fresh and interesting element to your shared story.

When Values Change

As people grow and change, so do relationships. Being ready to embrace these changes and grow with your partner is an important part of maintaining a long-lasting and healthy relationship. Change happens for all sorts of reasons, and can be both good and bad. Quitting smoking or starting to go to the gym, for example, are great positive changes that should be encouraged.

Major changes might include:

- Getting a job offer or wanting to move abroad
- A change in sexual preference
- Wanting/no longer wanting children
- Mental or physical health issues
- Exploring new beliefs or religions
- Redefining gender identities

Minor changes might include:

- A new friend or work colleague
- Being busier or unemployed
- New hobbies
- New habits

How to Deal With Change

Change, whether good or bad, can be a bit daunting. Processing changes within a relationship requires both individuals to be conscious of whatever change is taking place, and the potential impacts it might have on their well-being, as well as their relationship with their partner.

Identify the Reasons Behind the Change: Communicate with your partner and identify the reasons behind the change. There might not well be any – some people might just change their mind about having children, for example. However, someone who is suddenly exhibiting a change in behavior or acting out might be going through mental health issues, in which case investigating the reasons behind this change are important.

Define What Dealbreakers Are for You: If big changes are impacting your relationship beyond the degree to which you are comfortable, consider what your dealbreakers are. Maybe you are not ready to move abroad, have children, open your relationship, etc.

Change is a natural element of relationships, and you should try and embrace your relationship evolution and the compromise that it might require. As long as both you and your partner are willing to work together, you can come together as two individuals who bring out the best in one another, rather than letting go or losing yourself.

Relationship Evolution

Relationships tend also to naturally evolve, in a way that has been generally categorized into the five following stages:

Infatuation: Sometimes known as the 'honeymoon' phase, partners generally experience intense attraction and passion, and might idealize one another. Both partners are on their best behavior and may overlook any negative traits the other exhibits, as well as hide their own.

Merging: Taking it to the next level, couples might 'go official' and begin blending their lives.

Reality and Disillusionment: Both partners get a more realistic insight into the other, and might start to engage in a power struggle to navigate each other's differences as they are more comfortable with one another. Disagreements and conflict might arise, as well as doubts.

Commitment: Those able to work through their differences and collaborate on their love move on to a stage of commitment and mutual respect. They learn to accept differences and are better equipped to handle challenges thrown at them by life.

Co-Creation: In a truly bonded team, long-term partners form a dedicated and healthy bond with one another, and are more likely to stay together as their relationship strengthens over time.

Conflict #6: Working Through Issues With Outside Relationships

Now, you are head over heels for your partner. But you have a hard time with their mother or father. Or maybe they have a particularly nasty aunt, or a friend who you feel is trying to sabotage your relationship. Navigating extended relationships can at times be difficult, but is a big part of managing to merge your life with your partner's.

1. If You Do Not Like Your Partner's Friends

Get a gut feeling that one of your partner's friends has bad intentions and has a despicable influence on your partner? Or maybe you do not see eye to eye with their childhood friend, who keeps admonishing you or your parenting style and is spinning some pretty weird ideas to your kids. Having issues with your partner's loved ones is difficult, as ideally, you will form a combined life and share those in your close circle. However, if you feel yourself at odds with someone your partner considers a valuable connection, consider the following:

Talk to Your Partner: Obviously, do not start trash-talking your partner's loved ones without reason. However, if someone is making you uncomfortable or you sense an issue, communicate this to your partner so that they can support you and be mindful of future interactions.

Be Open to Getting to Know Them Better: Some people you just will not mesh with, but it is still worth being open-minded and giving bonding a shot when it comes to friends whom you do not instantly connect with.

Do Not Let It Impact Your Relationship: Try not to let outside relationships affect your relationship with your partner. Set boundaries when necessary to avoid interactions if that is what you need, but remember that your partner is separate from their friends, so you do not need to cut ties just because you do not get on with one of their loved ones.

2. If Your Partner's Friends Do Not Like You

Equally difficult is navigating the feeling that your partner's friends and family have taken an active dislike of you. It can make you feel closed off from your partner, and you might start to doubt your ability to continue your relationship if you feel unwelcome by your partner's close circle. However, this does not have to mean the end of your relationship. Not everyone will see eye to eye, and in the cases where you do feel like someone your partner considers a friend is showing aversion to you, consider the following:

Talk to Your Partner: As above, if you feel like someone in your partner's close circle has a problem with you, talk to your partner about it. They will be able to support you, mediate the situation, and help you navigate future interactions.

Try Not to Take It Personally: If someone does come into conflict with you, try not to take it personally. People come with all forms of triggers and reasons for their feelings. One of their friends might just be very protective and stand-offish, meaning it has nothing to do with you. A different friend might just be a sensitive and abrasive individual. The reasons for disliking someone can be vast and are often not down to your behavior.

Set Boundaries: If you find yourself coming into conflict with a particular individual in your partner's circle, do not be afraid to set boundaries to avoid this happening. Take a step back and find solutions that mean you potentially do not come into contact with that individual as much.

3. If Your Family Does Not Like Your Partner

You have gone public with your relationship. You have worked up the courage to bring them home and introduce them to your parents. But something is amiss. Your parents constantly criticize your partner, or they shut you down whenever you talk about your partner. They exclude your partner from invitations or tell you that they are not good enough for you. It is a very tricky situation to navigate, but be mindful of any prejudices your parents might hold. Use your knowledge of your parents and their beliefs to help try and assimilate them, using the below pointers:

Reiterate How Much You Value Your Partner: Show your parents how much you love and value your partner. Even if they hold their impressions, try and demonstrate the characteristics you hold dear and how much the ability of your family to get on with your partner means to you.

Be Open to Your Parent's Perspective: Do not be closed off to outside perspectives who might be able to see the red flags you are ignoring. It is easy to get blindsided by love, and your parents may well just be concerned for your well-being, having noticed alarming habits in your partner that you are not aware of.

Do Not Feel Forced to Choose Between Parents or Partner: While you might try and improve the relationship between your partner and your parents, you can ultimately set boundaries to avoid overly involving your partner with your parents. It is okay to continue healthy relationships with both, separately.

Questions for When Your Parents Do Not Like Your Partner:

Have your parents expressed any specific concerns regarding your partner?

_____

_____

_____

Are there any underlying reasons for this disapproval that you can think of, perhaps a misunderstanding, previous experiences, or cultural differences?

_____

_____

_____

How do these concerns make you feel?

_____

_____

_____

How might these issues be impacting your partner? Have you discussed this with them?

_____

_____

_____

_____

Are there any ways you might involve your partner and your parents in a positive activity?

_____

_____

_____

_____

If not, are there any boundaries you might be able to create to ensure your partner feels comfortable and supported, as do your parents, and you can continue having a healthy relationship with both?

_____

_____

_____

_____

4. If Your Partner's Family Does Not Like You

Maybe you are on the receiving end. You find that their mother rolls her eyes at whatever you say or comments on what you eat. Their father ignores you whenever you speak and belittles you, and the situation is unbearable. Having difficulties with your partner's family is a difficult situation to navigate, especially if you feel the need to go above and beyond to try and win them over, or feel disconnected from your partner as a result. If this applies to you, consider the following:

Try and Build a Positive Relationship With Them: If you do feel underlying tension, communicate with your partner and try and find ways to build a positive relationship with their family.

This is not always possible. In situations where you simply cannot work past an abrasive relationship with your partner's parents, communicate this issue with your partner, stand up for yourself, and know when to step back.

Consider How Much Involvement You Want in Their Lives: Should you experience a heightened degree of tension with your partner's parents, consider drawing boundaries around how much involvement you have with one another. Do not force your partner to take sides, but make sure that they are aware of how you feel, how you are being treated, and what the best way forwards is.

Questions for When Your Partner's Parents Do Not Like You:

What makes you feel that your partner's parents do not approve of you or like you?

_____

_____

_____

Are there any underlying reasons for this disapproval that you can think of, perhaps a misunderstanding, previous experiences, or cultural differences?

_____

_____

_____

_____

How do these concerns make you feel?

_____

_____

_____

_____

Have you discussed your feelings with your partner? Are there any ways in which they can work to support you?

_____

_____

_____

_____

Are there any ways you might be able to engage in positive activities or experiences with your partner's parents to build a stronger relationship?

_____

_____

_____

_____

If not, what boundaries might you set to help you maintain your well-being and protect your relationship respectfully?

_____

_____

_____

Activities:

1. Letter to Your Younger Self

It sounds cheesy, but sitting down and writing a letter to 'little you' can often be a great way to open up and reflect on your childhood. Particularly if you struggle with forming and maintaining healthy attachments, or are experiencing issues elsewhere in your relationships. If you consider yourself as carrying any trauma, this is also a great exercise for diving deeper into those emotions, if you are ready, and beginning to work through them.

When writing, consider what your aspirations were as a child:

Who did you want to be?

What was your family like at the time?

What advice would you give yourself, looking back?

What would younger you think of where you are in the world now?

---

2. Emotional Regulation

It can be easy to get overwhelmed and to focus on the negative aspects of things. These can morph and grow in our minds, and you can quickly turn a small annoyance into a colossal issue that takes up so much of your thought space that it becomes difficult to assess the situation from a rational perspective. Being in charge of your thoughts is a term that is thrown around quite often, but it is easier said than done. However, below are some exercises that can help you regulate your emotions and begin to harness how you see and feel things.

Checking In

If you do find your thoughts spiraling over something your partner has said or done, consider taking a step back and asking yourself the following questions to assess whether or not you are acting appropriately, or letting your thoughts get the better of you.

What am I angry/sad/upset about?

_____

_____

_____

What is the narrative that I am telling myself regarding what has happened?

_____

_____

_____

Are my feelings proportionate to the situation? Or am I letting my attachment style, past, or my interpretation influence my reaction?

_____

_____

_____

_____

_____

_____

Playing Opposites

You might have played it as a child. Someone says dog, you say cat. Someone says left, and you say right. When you are tempted to react in a certain way, particularly when feeling emotionally reactive, trying to approach the situation and your feelings from a completely different angle can be helpful. It is difficult. You cannot instantly snap out of being angry or depressed to elated and joyful, but gradually working on being able to control your emotions and change your internal narrative will greatly help regulate your emotions and benefit your relationship with your partner.

For example, if you are angry with your partner and want to text them continually or phone them to berate them, consider putting your phone aside for a few hours and going offline to distract yourself.

If you are anxious because your partner is on a work trip and want to check in with them constantly for reassurance, try and remind yourself of all the ways they have reassured you in the past, and how they have made you feel loved and secure.

Try it out for yourself:

What thoughts am I experiencing?

_____

_____

_____

_____

_____

How am I tempted to react to my emotions?

_____

_____

_____

_____

What might I do instead to reverse my initial reaction?

_____

_____

_____

_____

Grounding

When emotions do get the better of you, particularly anxiety, grounding methods can be incredibly helpful to self-soothe and regulate your emotions. Even if you do need to check back in with your partner to resolve conflict or address a situation, approaching this with a calm mind will benefit you both.

The 5-4-3-2-1 method is one of the most commonly used for anxiety. This helps you deflect your attention from whatever is causing your emotional upheaval and shifts your thoughts away from present anxiousness to a sense of calm and stability.

Start by taking a deep breath.

1.   Look around the room or space and identify 5 things you can see around you. You do not have to announce these. Your partner might think you are losing it if you do, but feel free to still get vocal if it helps.

2.   Now, try and pick out 4 things you could touch and consider their sensations. Your cat's fur, the wood of the table, the smoothness of a mirror, or a fluffy jumper.

3.   Continue to try and find 3 things you can hear. Maybe it is your fridge humming, birds chirping, or an ambulance in the distance.

4.   Try and pick out 2 things you can smell. Here is where it gets a bit more difficult, and hopefully concentrating on the smells around you will help ease your anxious thoughts. Can you smell freshly cut grass? Or maybe a candle?

5.   Lastly, try and think of 1 thing you can taste. This is usually the hardest, so if there is no taste of coffee or gum lingering in your mouth, think of something tasty and try and imagine how it would taste in your mouth.

A Heartfelt Request

Dear Reader,

I hope that the journey through my book has offered valuable insights and tools for enhancing your relationship. Whether it's deepening trust, improving communication, or strengthening intimacy, every step you take toward a healthier relationship can make a significant difference. Just as you have benefited from the shared wisdom within these pages, your unique perspective can guide others on their journey. By leaving an honest and genuine review on Amazon, you can help others find the resources they need to enhance their relationships. As an author, your feedback is vital. It helps me understand your experience as a reader and improves the success and reach of my work. Whether you found the book helpful, have suggestions for improvement, or want to share your own experiences, every word counts.

Scan to leave a review !

Rest assured, your review will be read and greatly appreciated. Positive or otherwise, your thoughts matter immensely. Thank you for taking the time to provide your valuable feedback. I eagerly await reading your insights.

Warm regards,

Chloe Slater

Conclusion

Congratulations on finishing this couples therapy workbook. Whether you are currently experiencing relationship struggles and are trying to resolve them, are trying to learn how to love your partner better and how to communicate effectively, or are just generally looking to improve and educate yourself on how to maintain a healthy relationship, I hope you leave with a more confident and positive outlook.

Love is challenging at times. It comes with immense highs and lows, many of which we have covered in this book. Even if they do not apply to you now, you will be more informed on what to look out for, and how to approach common issues that many couples face, should they arise in your relationship.

If you are currently experiencing relationship conflict, you will be a step closer to resolving this with your partner using your newfound conflict resolution skills. Once you have incorporated your listening and communication skills, and to some degree compromised on your issues, you will also have the skills needed to rebuild trust and rekindle both emotional and intimate connections with your partner.

Relationships are marathons, not races. If you are in a period of struggling, remind yourself that every couple goes through bouts of conflict and variations in how they feel toward one another. You are by no means alone in this, and the best thing is that you have a partner with whom you can collaboratively work through these struggles.

Remember: you are a team. Work together, continue to incorporate the activities mentioned in the book into your daily life, such as check-ins, bonding exercises, and reflections, and have faith that putting effort into your relationship can bring you both a lifetime of happiness.

About the Author

A remarkable figure in the sphere of relationship dynamics, Chloe Slater stands as a beacon of understanding and mutual growth for countless individuals and couples worldwide. Her insightful and approachable style has made her a respected voice, bringing clarity and practical solutions to complex relational challenges.

Chloe's journey into the intricacies of human connections began at a personal level. Observing, exploring, and questioning her own experiences, she cultivated an ability to recognize patterns and behaviors that underpin relationship dynamics. This personal exploration gradually developed into a focused interest, shedding light on the rich tapestry of human interactions and the bonds they form. Over time, Chloe has fine-tuned her understanding of the principles that make relationships thrive. She has delved into the mechanics of emotional awareness, effective communication, and mutual empathy, applying these insights to offer practical guidance for relationship enhancement.

Chloe's unique approach, rooted in real-world experiences and a deep understanding of human nature, has cemented her role as a transformative figure in the field of relationship coaching. Her dedication to providing relatable, insightful guidance for a broad spectrum of relationships has resonated with many, leading to a broad and growing audience.

Away from her professional pursuits, Chloe is an avid reader, immersing herself in books that widen her perspectives and challenge her thoughts. She finds solace and inspiration in nature, often taking long, reflective walks to reset and rejuvenate. She cherishes family time, believing that the everyday interactions and quiet moments are where life's most profound lessons lie. Chloe continues her quest for knowledge and understanding, fueled by her passion to help others cultivate deeper connections and find fulfillment in their relationships.

Made in the USA
Las Vegas, NV
16 September 2023

77620513R00096